# Music and Tradition

# Music and Tradition

*Essays on Asian and other musics presented to Laurence Picken*

Edited by D. R. WIDDESS and R. F. WOLPERT

**Cambridge University Press**

CAMBRIDGE
LONDON NEW YORK NEW ROCHELLE
MELBOURNE SYDNEY

Published by the Press Syndicate of the University of Cambridge
The Pitt Building, Trumpington Street, Cambridge CB2 1RP
32 East 57th Street, New York, NY 20011, USA
296 Beaconsfield Parade, Middle Park, Melbourne 3206, Australia

First published 1981

Typeset by Ward Partnership, Widdington, Essex
Printed in Great Britain at the University Press, Cambridge

*Library of Congress Cataloguing in Publication Data*
Main entry under title:
Music and tradition.
    Includes bibliographical references.
    CONTENTS: Condit, J. Two Song-dynasty Chinese
tunes preserved in Korea. – Marett, A. "Banshiki
Sangun" and "Shōenraku". – Wolpert, R. Tang-music
(Tōgaku) manuscripts for lute and their interrelation-
ships. [etc.]
    1. Music – Asia – Addresses, essays, lectures.
2. Music – Addresses, essays, lectures. 3. Picken,
Laurence. I. Picken, Laurence. II. Wolpert, R.F.
III. Widdess, D.R.
ML55.P52 1979    781.7′5    78-73235
ISBN 0 521 22400 4

# Contents

# Preface

This volume is a collection of essays on various aspects of (primarily) Asian musics, which we hope may be of interest to the general musical reader as well as to specialists in the different areas covered. The stimulus that brought these items together is a personal one: the occasion of Laurence Picken's seventieth birthday provides a welcome opportunity to say 'Congratulations', and 'Thank you'.

Ten years ago, internationally distinguished scholars in the field of ethnomusicology celebrated Laurence Picken's sixtieth birthday by preparing a similar volume (*Perspectives on Asian Musics*, published as volume VI, numbers 1 and 2 (1975), of the American journal *Asian Music*), in which they 'joined in applauding his outstanding achievements in Oriental musicology'. The account of his distinguished careers in zoology, biology and musicology presented there need not be repeated. Since 1969, the stream of his publications, including his monumental *The folk musical instruments of Turkey* (Oxford 1975), has not abated. But much of his energy in the past ten years has been devoted to teaching, encouraging and collaborating with students and colleagues in the study of Asian and other musics, especially in Cambridge. Three of the contributors to this volume participated in a 'Tang music project' financed by the Andrew Mellon Foundation; four more pupils have pursued or are pursuing research in other fields under his guidance; distinguished scholars from overseas come to Cambridge to consult or collaborate with him; and an interest in non-Western musics has been kindled and encouraged in many, directly or indirectly, by his presence here over the years. He has recently undertaken the editing of a new journal, *Musica Asiatica*, in which the work of his research group is appearing; and serial publication of a complete edition of *Music from the Tang court* (Oxford, forthcoming) is in hand.

The University of Cambridge owes him a special debt: on retiring from his position as Assistant Director of Research (Oriental Music) in the Faculty of Oriental Studies in 1976, he presented his extensive collection of books on Oriental and other musics, together with an important collection of Tōgaku part-books, to the University Library. These collections, and the large collection of musical instruments from all over the world that was acquired from him by the University at the same time, together constitute one of the most valuable resources for teaching and research in non-Western musics in this country.

It is as an expression of gratitude and appreciation, from some of those who have most directly benefited (and continue to benefit) from these activities, that this volume was conceived. As a result, all the contributions that follow, to greater and lesser extents, reflect Laurence Picken's own approaches and interests. Three concerns may be said to characterise his writings and teaching. First, a conception of musicology as a *science*, involving 'the recognition of correlations, their exploration, their use in prediction; the questioning of material in the light of hypotheses', a concept reflected, for example, in his meticulously precise use of language. Secondly, a preoccupation with history, especially those remote periods of history that are still present to us in the high civilisations of the East and in folk cultures everywhere. Thirdly, and most important, an intense delight in music of almost every kind — from Philippine bamboo-zither music to *Die Kunst der Fuge* — and for its own sake.

This overriding interest in 'real music' has produced transcriptions and analyses of the earliest Chinese music that survives in notation, including both ritual and entertainment music of the Tang dynasty, and the sacred and secular songs of the Song-dynasty poet Jiang Kui (A.D. 1155—1229). It also manifests itself in the importance Laurence Picken places on practical experiment. Those of us studying early sources of notation under his guidance will recall with gratitude and pleasure the many informal gatherings at which we have played together, on an *ad hoc* mixture of Oriental and Occidental instruments, whatever music we were individually working on at the time. Such occasions provide one with the acid test for theories, insights into the practicalities of musical performance, a stimulating interchange of ideas, and hours of musical enjoyment (in one series of such meetings, almost the entire Tōgaku repertory was played through from eleventh-century and later part-books). The court musicians of mediaeval China, Korea, Japan and India would be surprised, no doubt, to hear our renditions, but gratified, surely, at the pleasure their music continues to give.

The essays in this book concern the music and musical instruments of Japan, Korea, China, Burma, Central Asia, India, The Gambia, and Anglo-Saxon England, and cover a time-scale from the fifth century A.D. to the present day. Their diversity reflects the enthusiasm for many aspects of world music that Laurence Picken has encouraged in a wide circle of pupils, colleagues and friends. They do not, however, attempt to explore every aspect of 'music and tradition'. In particular, consideration of the social environment, ultimately essential for the understanding of any musical tradition, is for the most part left on one side. Rather, most contributions (except the organological ones) examine a particular tradition, with special attention to particular items of repertory (presented in transcription), and draw conclusions about the workings of the musical language or its historical development. The book is therefore addressed primarily to those whose interest is in musical structures and their development, rather than in social and historical perspectives.

While almost all music arises in the context of a 'tradition', we are primarily concerned with musical cultures in which tradition, rather than the individual, is a predominant force in the generation of music. As Bartók pointed out, in cultures where the individual 'composer', as we know him in the West, has a smaller (if any) rôle to play, where 'originality' is not the prime criterion, and where the repertory is preserved in the memory of musicians rather than in writing, it is the gradual transformation of traditional melodies by successive generations of performers that leads to the development of 'new' music: music which, in Bartók's view, occupies a 'peak of artistic perfection' as a result of centuries of refinement. However, since notation is not normally used in such cultures, one can rarely observe the process at work over any great length of time. Exceptions are to be found in traditions such as those of Japan and Korea, where notation has been used for many centuries to record the practice of successive generations of performers (who nevertheless remained primarily loyal to their memories and musical instincts rather than to the notation). In the court-music traditions of Japan and Korea, as in the solo tradition of the Chinese qin, the force of tradition has kept the same 'pieces' in the repertory for many centuries. Thus the court musicians of Japan claim to preserve the entertainment music of the Tang Chinese court, imported into Japan before the end of the ninth century A.D. – a claim which Laurence Picken has shown to be at least partly justified. But at the same time, the instinct for variation and embellishment has apparently led, in both Japan and Korea, to a radical transformation: there is now nothing that sounds 'Chinese' about Japanese court-music, or about those items of the Korean court repertory that are supposed to have been imported from China. In Japan, Laurence Picken would argue, the addition of embellishment, especially in the flute (ryūteki) and reed-pipe (hichiriki) parts, has been accompanied by a massive reduction in the speed of performance, so that the melody – presented as a less elaborate 'cantus firmus' in the lute, zither and mouth-organ parts – moves too slowly to be heard as such. Today, the elaborated flute and reed-pipe parts are considered to be 'the melody'. In Korea, it seems that all instruments have participated equally in the process of elaboration, and the sequence of sources discussed by Jonathan Condit, in this volume and elsewhere, demonstrates the successive encrustations of new material with which the original melodies have become endowed.

Laurence Picken's view of the development of the Tang-music repertory in Japan is, as yet, far from being generally accepted. In tracing many of the original melodies through China to prototypes in Central Asia, he confirms the traditional account of the origins of this music, according to which it was brought as exotic tribute to the Tang capital from the West. But in regarding the melodies of the mouth-organ and lute part-books as the 'basic tunes', of which the modern wind parts are 'elaborated versions', he challenges the traditional view of Japanese scholars, and hence of most others, according to whom the mouth-organ, zither and lute parts are 'simplified' versions of the flute and reed-pipe 'melodies'. Despite the evidence of the early manuscripts, the belief that the music has not materially changed since the Tang dynasty is still widely held.

In the present volume, Rembrandt Wolpert shows that the written lute parts have indeed remained essentially unchanged, either in content or in method of notation, since the twelfth century. However, the character of the melodies, as revealed in his transcriptions, implies a much brisker tempo than that adopted today. Allan Marett, examining the earliest surviving flute-score (A.D. 966), concludes that the metrical complexities of the suite 'Banshiki Sangun' (which is no longer played today) would have been imperceptible unless performed at a similarly faster speed. Jonathan Condit, tracing the development of two eleventh-century Chinese melodies in the Korean court repertory up to the present day, provides substantial evidence for a process of progressive retardation and elaboration parallel to that believed to have occurred in Japan. A forthcoming study of Japanese court song (Saibara) by Elizabeth Markham (who was unfortunately unable to contribute to the present volume) will investigate a third example of the same kind of process, whereby the original tenth-century or earlier melodies have become metrically distorted, and overlaid with vocal figurations probably derived from Buddhist chant – developments which are presumed to reflect a reduction in tempo.

Also in this volume, Yoko Mitani discusses aspects of the music of the Chinese long-zither qin, a solo instrument for which melodies have been 'preserved' since legendary times. Here personal interpretation is of paramount importance: hence the notation provides a melodic skeleton only, allowing the performer considerable freedom especially in the matter of rhythm. Richard Widdess and Lucy Durán examine traditions in which notation has a smaller part, if any, to play, and in which 'improvisation' constitutes an important element in any performance. In both North Indian vocal music and in Mandinka kora music, improvisation is based on traditional materials – tunings, modes, rhythmic patterns, 'composed' melodies – and takes place within traditional formal structures. Where there is written evidence, as in India, it appears that such forms may remain relatively unchanged for several centuries. The importance of the individual performer is illustrated by an item from a master kora-player's repertory, in which improvised 'variation' is based on several interrelated 'themes', some old, some new.

The last three contributions explore the early history of three types of stringed instrument: bowed lutes, harps, and lyres. Harvey Turnbull discusses the use of plectra, friction-sticks and bows on lutes in ancient Central Asia and elsewhere; Muriel Williamson reviews all the iconographic evidence that has so far come to light for the history of the arched harp in Burma; and Graeme Lawson discusses the relationship between early European harps and lyres.

Our joint thanks go to all those whose labours have made the book possible: especially to Elizabeth Markham and Margaret Widdess, for their assistance in preparing materials for the press; to Francesca Bray, Puka Wolpert and Yi Chae-Suk, for help with Chinese characters and romanisation; to Mr R.S. Wang, for drawing the characters; and to Clare Davies-Jones and Eric Van Tassel of the Cambridge University Press, for their understanding and help.

R.F.W.                                                D.R.W.

Peterhouse                                         Christ's College

Cambridge                                         Cambridge

# Note on romanisation

Chinese words and names have been romanised according to the pinyin system throughout this book, except in the case of a few personal names. Characters for Chinese, Japanese and Korean words and names are given where necessary in a glossary at the end of each article. The glossaries also include Wade-Giles romanisation of certain well-known terms (for example, names of musical instruments). Chinese and Japanese characters are also given where appropriate in the bibliography appended to each article.

# Two Song-dynasty Chinese tunes preserved in Korea

JONATHAN CONDIT

## I. Introduction

During the Tang and Song dynasties (seventh to thirteenth centuries), Chinese music was imported into Korea and performed at the court. The magnitude of the importation can be judged from the fact that the court repertoire was divided into two categories — 'Chinese music' (*Tangak*) and 'native music' (*hyangak*) — each with its own separate corps of musicians. After the fall of Song the importation ceased, but the Chinese pieces which were already in repertoire continued to be performed. The *History of Koryŏ* (*Koryŏ-sa*)[1] preserves the titles and song-texts of more than forty pieces imported from Song (that they were imported from Song and not Tang can be known from the poetic form of the texts). Of these, two are still performed today: 'Walking in the Void' ('Pohŏja') and 'Spring in Luoyang' ('Nagyangch'un').

    Although the two pieces are Chinese in origin, they have undergone such radical change in Korea that it would be inaccurate to consider them 'Chinese' as they are now performed. Fortunately, the history of the pieces can be traced through surviving scores of the fifteenth to nineteenth centuries. Consideration of the two pieces will be divided into two parts. In the first

---

1  The Koryŏ dynasty ruled Korea from 918 to 1392.

part, the original tunes will be restored on the basis of the earliest versions of the pieces in the surviving scores; in the second part, the history of the tunes in the Korean court repertoire will be traced from the fifteenth century to the present day. It gives me particular pleasure to publish this essay in Dr Picken's honour, for the findings presented here are at once a pendant to his masterly studies on the surviving Chinese scores for Song music (1957, 1966, 1969a, 1971a), and an extension of his seminal work on the Gagaku tradition of Japanese court music (1967, 1969b, 1971b, 1974, 1977), in which he established that the Chinese music imported into Japan has undergone profound change, but that the original tunes are still recoverable.

## II. Restoration of the original tunes

### (a) 'Walking in the Void'

The two earliest surviving versions of 'Walking in the Void' (hereafter cited as WV) date from the sixteenth century. One is found in *Zither Tablature Book* (*Kŭm hapcha-bo*, 1572; hereafter *ZTB*); the other is included in *Latter Book of Great Music* (*Taeak hubo*; hereafter *LBGM*), a collection of pieces from the fifteenth to seventeenth centuries compiled in 1759. (*LBGM* does not indicate either the date or the source of any of its pieces.) Judging from their similarity in musical idiom, the two versions are of approximately the same date. *ZTB* has parts for flute, kŏmun'go,[2] and drum; *LBGM* has parts for kŏmun'go and drum. Both scores also include the original song-text. The kŏmun'go parts (with song-text in Sino-Korean) are illustrated in Example 1.[3]

Example 1. WV, bars 5–8: *ZTB* (1572) and *LBGM* (sixteenth century)

---

2 A 'half-tube' zither with six strings, three of which (II, III, IV) pass over a series of sixteen frets, and the remaining three of which (I, V, VI) are supported on movable bridges. II and III function as melody strings, I, IV, V, VI as drone strings. Plucked with a cylindrical bamboo stick. Regarded as the noblest of Korean instruments. The great majority of surviving Korean scores are for the kŏmun'go. Most of the music examined here will be kŏmun'go parts for pieces played by ensembles including other plucked string instruments as well as winds and bowed strings; the other parts would have been heterophonically related to the kŏmun'go part.

3 In transcribing *ZTB* and other kŏmun'go parts, auxiliary signs relating to plucking and finger techniques are ignored in order to facilitate reading (*LBGM* includes no such signs).

Two points suggest that these versions of WV are far removed from the original tune. First, there are only three syllables of text for four bars of music. With the text delivered so slowly, it would be difficult, if not impossible, to follow the sense of the poem. Most likely, in the original tune there were fewer notes per syllable of text. Second, these versions are in 12/8 – a metre very common in Korea but virtually unknown in China. There is reason to suspect, then, that by the sixteenth century the original tune had already been transformed at the hands of Korean musicians.

The piece directly preceding WV in *ZTB* is 'Giving the People Joy' ('Yŏmillak'), another piece of Chinese origin.[4] *ZTB*'s 'Giving the People Joy' (hereafter GPJ) is in the same musical style as *ZTB*'s WV. Fortunately for our purposes, an earlier and much simpler version of GPJ is preserved in the *Veritable Records of Sejong* (*Sejong sillok*, 1454; hereafter *Sejong*). Example 2 shows the relationship between the two versions. The versions are a minor third apart in key, but this conveniently means that corresponding notes appear at the same positions in treble and bass clefs.

Example 2. GPJ: corresponding excerpts from *Sejong* (1454) and *ZTB* (1572)

*Sejong*'s version is consonant with the Chinese musical tradition in both rhythmic and melodic style, and certainly does not sound Korean. Furthermore, the number of notes per syllable of text is more reasonable than in *ZTB*'s version. *Sejong*'s GPJ, if not itself a Chinese version of the tune, is clearly much closer to the original Chinese version of GPJ than is *ZTB*'s version. The relationship between the two versions shows that, in the evolution of GPJ, each beat (crotchet) in *Sejong* becomes a bar of 12/8 in *ZTB*. Despite the great rhythmic expansion, however, *ZTB* maintains a very close melodic relationship to *Sejong*: *Sejong*'s melodic contour is preserved, with the addition of simple ornamentation.

Since *ZTB*'s versions of GPJ and WV are the same in musical style, we may surmise that WV underwent the same process of evolution as GPJ. That is, *ZTB*'s WV must derive from a much simpler fifteenth-century version in 4/4. Such a version is easy to restore on the basis of *ZTB*'s version. It is to be noted that bar 5 of *ZTB*'s WV (Example 1) is exactly the same as bar 138 of *ZTB*'s GPJ (Example 2). We may therefore suppose that the corresponding *beat* of the hypothetical fifteenth-century version of WV is the same as the second beat in bar 35 (i.e. beat 138)

4   Although of Chinese origin, 'Giving the People Joy' is here treated only incidentally, because (a) the original Chinese song-text has been lost (the surviving text is a Korean composition), and (b) the structure of the tune may have been changed when the new text was fitted to the music. For the history of this piece, see Condit 1977.

of *Sejong*'s GPJ. *ZTB*'s WV has a total of forty-four bars; of these, twenty-two separate bars are identical to separate bars in GPJ. Hence, in restoring the fifteenth-century version of WV, we may simply substitute those beats from *Sejong*'s GPJ which correspond to the matching bars in WV. As shown in Example 3, bars 5 and 6 of *ZTB*'s WV are the same as bars 138 and 40 of *ZTB*'s GPJ. Therefore, beats 5 and 6 of the fifteenth-century version of WV were most likely the same as beats 138 and 40 of *Sejong*'s GPJ.

Example 3. Restoration of a bar of the fifteenth-century version of WV on the basis of correspondences between *ZTB*'s WV and GPJ

Of WV's bars which are not exactly the same, most are closely related to bars of GPJ. In Example 3, bar 8 of *ZTB*'s WV is closely related to bar 28 of *ZTB*'s GPJ. The first half of the bar is the same melodic figure at a higher pitch-level (the difference in interval is due to the structure of the pentatonic scale), and the second half of the bar is identical to the second half of GPJ's bar. Hence beat 8 of the fifteenth-century version of WV is the same as beat 28 of *Sejong*'s GPJ, except that the first note is one step higher in the pentatonic scale. The few bars of WV which do not resemble any bar from GPJ can be plausibly reduced from a bar of 12/8 to a beat of 4/4 without difficulty. In Example 3, bar 7 of *ZTB*'s WV clearly derives from a pair of quavers: d″ c″. With the restoration of this beat, one bar of the fifteenth-century version of WV is complete. This bar is musically plausible. Like *Sejong*'s GPJ, the bar is consonant with the Chinese musical tradition, and displays a reasonable ratio of notes to syllables of text.

The restoration of the fifteenth-century version of WV is carried out in its entirety in Example 4. Indication is given of which bars are exactly the same as (=) or closely related to (~) a bar from *ZTB*'s GPJ. For the sake of comparison, both sixteenth-century versions (*ZTB* and *LBGM*) are given. For reasons to be explained below, *LBGM*'s version includes a slightly varied repeat of bars 9–31. In the four instances where the repeat of a bar differs from its first occurrence, the repeat is also given. The text is laid out under the restored fifteenth-century version. The portion of the text that appears in Example 4 comprises the first five of the poem's eight lines; the fate of the missing three lines is considered below.

Example 4. Restoration of the fifteenth-century version of WV

Several points in the relationship between the sixteenth-century versions and the fifteenth-century version call for comment. For bars 9 and 21 of the sixteenth-century versions, I have followed *LBGM* rather than *ZTB* in restoring the fifteenth-century version. Although *LBGM* is in general somewhat more elaborately ornamented than *ZTB*, the former curiously preserves two bars of the fifteenth-century version with no added ornamentation whatever, in the repeat of bars 13–14. At two places in the sixteenth-century versions the original pitch-level is transposed up an octave (*ZTB*, *LBGM*: bars 31–2; *ZTB*: bars 37–44). In the fifteenth-century version the lower pitch-level has been restored. The only point at which *ZTB* and *LBGM* differ sufficiently to warrant giving alternative restorations is bar 32: *ZTB*'s bar 32 clearly derives from a crotchet b♭, while *LBGM*'s bar 32 as clearly derives from quavers c′ b♭.

The restored fifteenth-century version is plausible as a tune, and has a consistent musical character of its own. One respect in which this version differs notably from surviving tunes of the Song dynasty, however, is the degree of ornamentation. The Song tunes are set almost exclusively one note to one syllable, with only occasional descending or ascending 'liquescent neumes', as in Example 5. In contrast, the fifteenth-century version of WV sets as many as eight notes to one syllable (Example 4, bars 3 and 6). Furthermore, the large number of repeated

Lu  si  di  fu  Yuan-yang  Pu.  Xiang Tao - ye  dang  shi  huan  du.

You jiang chou  yan  yu  chun feng.  Tai  qu.  Qi  lan rao  geng  shao  zhu.

Example 5. First stanza of Jiang Kui's second secular song (as transcribed by Picken, 1966)

notes within the compass of one syllable of text (Example 4, bar 2, beat 1; bar 3, beat 1; bar 4, beats 3–4; etc.) suggests that the fifteenth-century version is an ornamented version for instruments, rather than the original tune as sung by the voice. In light of the great difference between the fifteenth- and sixteenth-century versions of WV, it is only prudent to assume that, since the tune was introduced into Korea no later than the thirteenth century (the fall of Song), the fifteenth-century version probably does not represent the original version of the tune. Hence we are justified in attempting to reduce the fifteenth-century version to an even simpler form.

The simplest possible version (and one that would accord with what we know of Song tunes) would have one note per syllable. In the fifteenth-century version, the syllables last either one or two beats. Each subdivided beat can easily be viewed as an ornamented crotchet – in other words, the 'main note' of each beat is easily identified. The ornaments are readily classifiable as turns, passing notes, auxiliary notes, anticipations, appoggiaturas, and échappées. In Example 6, the upper line gives the fifteenth-century version with each ornament labelled, and the lower line gives the simplest possible version with all ornaments stripped away.

The simplest possible version is attractive and plausible as a tune. (The last bar of Example 6 clearly cannot be the end of the tune, however.) Though lending itself to ornamentation, the

Example 6. WV: fifteenth-century version and simplest possible version
t = turn; p = passing note; aux = auxiliary note; ant = anticipation; app = appoggiatura; é = échappée

tune does not require ornamentation to be musically satisfying. Each syllable of text is set to either one or two notes; note-values are restricted to crotchet and minim. A strictly syllabic setting of the text would require reducing each pair of slurred crotchets to a minim on the pitch of one or other of the crotchets, but since this cannot be done without impairing the musical quality of the tune, I have retained the pairs of slurred notes. In general, the 'main note' of each subdivided beat is the first note (the two exceptions are the appoggiaturas on the last beat of bars 4 and 8). Each line of text is set to a two-bar phrase, except line 3, which fills a three-bar phrase with its greater length (ten syllables). With this version, we have reached the ultimate reduction of the surviving sixteenth-century Korean versions.

The final issue to be considered in relation to WV is the original formal structure of the tune. As mentioned above, the portion of the text that appears in Examples 4 and 6 comprises only the first five of the poem's original eight lines. These five lines comprise the first quatrain, plus the first line of the second quatrain:

first quatrain ⎡ line 1 = bars 1–2
               | line 2 = bars 3–4
               | line 3 = bars 5–7
               ⎣ line 4 = bars 8–9

second quatrain     line 1 = bars 10–11

The missing lines are therefore the last three lines of the second quatrain. Neither *ZTB* nor *LBGM* records the complete text, but a number of later sources do.[5] In all of these, the last three lines of the second quatrain are set to the same music as the last three lines of the first quatrain. Since the last three lines of the first quatrain are set to bars 3—9 in the original tune, we need simply add a repetition of these bars after bar 11. With this addition, the tune is fully restored to its original form. Example 7 gives the fully restored tune with the text in the original Chinese, in transliterated Sino-Korean, in a free English paraphrase, and in transliterated Chinese.[6]

Example 7. Original form of WV

5   Two untitled kŏmun'go scores (post-1610; Seoul National University Library microfilms 72-35-B and 72-36-J) and the *Newly Verified Zither Book* (*Sinjŭng kŭmbo*, ?1740).
6   The version of the text is that found in the *History of Koryŏ*, Book 71. Later sources (including *ZTB* and *LBGM*) have a slightly different version. The title 'Walking in the Void' is the name of the tune, to which any number of texts could be composed, rather than the name of this particular text.

The structure exemplified by this tune – repeated stanzas with a varied beginning for the first line of the second stanza – is found in the great majority of the music of Tang and Song which survives respectively in Japanese and Chinese sources (Picken 1966, 1969a, 1969b, 1971, 1974, 1977; Marett 1976, 1977; Wolpert 1975). It is to be noted that the second line of each verse is fitted to the same melodic phrase despite the difference in number of syllables (bars 3–4 and 12–13). With the addition of the repeated bars, it also becomes clear that the final cadence is on F, so the scale of the tune is F G A C D, with auxiliary note B♭. Such a mode – pentatonic, with a flattened auxiliary fourth degree – although different from the basic mode of Chinese music, the Lydian mode, with its sharp auxiliary fourth degree, is nevertheless in keeping with the Chinese musical tradition.

In sum, three points argue in favour of accepting Example 7 as the original tune known in Song dynasty China. (1) It has been reduced to the simplest possible level of ornamentation yet remains musically satisfying. (2) It has been arrived at by direct derivation from the earliest surviving Korean sources, using a reductive process based on the known evolution of the Korean musical tradition. (3) It accords with the surviving music of Song with respect to note–syllable ratio and structure, and with the Chinese musical tradition in general with respect to mode.

### (b) 'Spring in Luoyang'

The only surviving source for 'Spring in Luoyang' (henceforth SL) is *Source of Popular Music* (*Sogak wŏnbo*; henceforth *SPM*), a score printed in 1892. Like *LBGM*, *SPM* is a collection of pieces from earlier centuries. The score is divided into seven books, each book containing pieces in a uniform musical style and thus apparently of similar date. (Again, like *LBGM*, *SPM* indicates neither dates nor original sources for its pieces.) Book 4 of *SPM* comprises two pieces: GPJ (identical to *Sejong*'s version) and SL. Since the two pieces are similar in musical style and occur in the same book of *SPM*, we may conclude that *SPM*-4's SL is similar in date to *Sejong*'s GPJ – that is, fifteenth-century. *SPM*-4 gives the tune and percussion parts only, without the song-text. The text is preserved, however, in the *History of Koryŏ*, and has been convincingly refitted to the tune by Lee (1967: 77–113). The text is of particular interest as the work of a well-known Song poet, Ouyang Xiu (1007–72). Example 8 gives *SPM*-4's version with the text as restored by Lee.

SL shares several features with WV. The melodic style is similar to that of the restored fifteenth-century version of WV, with some of the same figures (compare, for example, SL bar 7, beat 4, with WV bar 2, beat 4). (SL, however, has none of the demisemiquaver turns so prominent in WV.) The structure comprises repeated verses with a varied beginning for the first line of the second verse. (*SPM*-4 indicates the repeat from bar 3, but fails to indicate the end of the piece, hence the brackets around '*fine*'.) The basic scale is 'F major' pentatonic (F G A C D), but in this case with the orthodox sharp auxiliary fourth degree of the Lydian mode (B♮) in bar 4. *SPM*-4 notates the auxiliary seventh degree in bar 9 as E♭ ; I have corrected it to E♮ to agree with modern performance (see pp. 27–30 below) and with the Lydian series. The syllables of text last either one or two beats.

Example 8. SL: *SPM*-4's version (*c.* 1450)

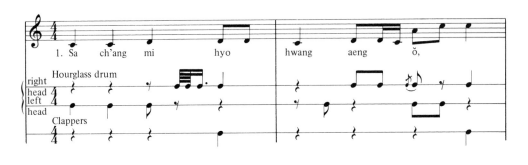

1. Sa ch'ang mi hyo hwang aeng ŏ,

Hourglass drum
right head
left head
Clappers

Hye ro so chan chu; Myŏn yu ra mak
(2) Yŏm mi san mu so; P'a hwa sik nu

[*Fine*]

to ch'un han, Chak ya ri sam kaeng u.
hyang kwi hong, Mun lae ch'ŏ pong nang pul.

*D.S.* % *al Fine*

2. Suk nyŏm han ŭi ch'wi kyŏng sŏ,

12

As with the restored fifteenth-century version of WV, *SPM*-4's SL frequently sets several notes to a syllable of text (the maximum being four, in bars 6 and 10). Once again, the 'main note' of each subdivided beat is easily identified, and ornaments are readily classifiable as passing notes, auxiliary notes, échappées, anticipations, turns, and appoggiaturas. By stripping away all ornaments, the simplest possible version is reached (Example 9).

The simplest possible version is again an attractive and plausible tune, with each syllable of text set to one or two notes. The melodic contour can be made still more attractive by trans-

Example 9. SL: *SPM*-4 and simplest possible version (cf. Example 6)

posing the first bar and a half of each verse up an octave.[7] If this is done, bars 2 and 10 become identical to bar 7, and the tune as a whole has a satisfying descending motion. Example 10 gives this revision of the simplest possible version, together with the text in the original Chinese, in transliterated Sino-Korean, in a free English paraphrase, and in transliterated Chinese (again, the title 'Spring in Luoyang' is the name of the tune, rather than the name of this particular text). It seems to me likely that this was the form of the tune known to Ouyang Xiu and his contemporaries in eleventh-century China.

Example 10. Probable original form of SL (the 'geese' in bar 14 are returning from a migration)

Having reached the simplest possible versions of both tunes, it is of interest to compare them with each other (Example 11).

7   I owe this suggestion to Dr Picken.

Example 11. Simplest possible versions of WV and SL

Two features shared by the tunes are particularly noteworthy: (1) Phrases 1, 2, and 4 (corresponding to lines 1, 2, and 4 of the text) are in the same rhythm in both tunes:

(Phrase 3 could not be in the same rhythm because the lines have differing numbers of syllables.) (2) The first bar of each couplet ends with two repeated notes (boxed in the example). These shared features are evident only in the simplest possible versions, and are not to be found in the fifteenth-century versions (compare Examples 6 and 9). This may be taken both as a confirmation of the validity of the simplest possible versions and as evidence that the tunes originated in the same historical period — perhaps the eleventh century (the time of Ouyang Xiu) — and in the same geographical region of China.

**(c) The two tunes in relation to the rhythm of Song tunes preserved in China**

WV and SL are particularly valuable in the study of Song music because they are recorded in a rhythmically explicit notation. In contrast, the Song music preserved in Chinese sources is recorded in a notation with only occasional rhythmic indications, and these are often of uncertain significance. Although the earliest surviving version of WV (*ZTB*) is quite far removed from the Chinese original, we may assume that the *relative* durations of the syllables of text have been faithfully retained. (The evidence in favour of this assumption is that the relative durations of the text-syllables in *Sejong*'s version of GPJ are retained in *ZTB*'s GPJ.) Hence, although it has been necessary to employ a process of reduction to recover the original tune of WV, the rhythm of the text may be accepted as a direct survival from Song, expanded in absolute duration but unchanged with respect to relative duration. This is, to my knowledge, the only such survival from the Song period. Since SL's text is missing in *SPM-4*, the rhythm of the text as restored by Lee, while totally convincing, cannot be taken as direct evidence regarding Song music. Nevertheless, since it is recorded in a rhythmically explicit notation, SL is valuable as an example of the musical structure to which a Song lyric is known to have been set. Once again, to my knowledge, SL is the only such surviving example.

In his transcriptions of Song music, Laurence Picken has found it necessary to make a series of assumptions regarding the probable rhythm of the tunes (1966). The key assumption, and the one from which the others flow, is that a seven-syllable line was sung to eight beats, the seventh syllable occupying the last two beats (Example 5, bars 1, 2, 3). WV includes two seven-syllable lines (Example 7, bars 1–2 and 10–11); both lines of text are delivered in the rhythm proposed:  ♩ ♩ ♩ ♩ · ♩ ♩ ♩ . Lee has also restored SL's seven-syllable lines in this rhythm (Example 10, bars 1–2, 5–6, 9–10, 13–14).

A consequence following from this assumption is that the standard poetic form of the Tang – the *jueju*, a quatrain of seven-syllable lines – would have been sung to a tune composed of four phrases of eight beats. During the Song, the jueju was superseded by the *ci*, a form with irregular line-lengths. As Picken has demonstrated, the shorter type of ci, known as *ling*, had approximately the same total number of syllables per stanza as a jueju. He therefore postulates that ling were sung to tunes with the same, or nearly the same, structure as tunes suitable for jueju – that is, tunes with four eight-beat phrases. SL and WV are both ling, and both are sung to tunes with the postulated structure: SL's verses each have four eight-beat phrases, and WV's verses have four and a half eight-beat phrases (the extra half-phrase is necessary to accommodate the ten syllables of lines 3 and 7).

Finally, since the lines of a ci are of differing lengths, they will necessarily be set in different rhythms. Theoretical writings of the period mention only three rhythmic values, which may be transcribed as minim, crotchet, and quaver. Picken points out that if only three rhythmic values are available, and if the lines (ranging in length from two to nine or more syllables) are to be set to eight-beat phrases (or four-beat phrases for the shorter lines), the number of possible rhythmic transcriptions is limited. Besides the seven-syllable lines, WV includes lines of five, six, and ten syllables; the five- and six-syllable lines are set as follows:

Both of these are among the rhythmic transcriptions used by Picken, as in Example 12. Lee also uses these same rhythms in fitting SL's five- and six-syllable lines to the tune. WV's ten-syllable lines are set in the rhythm:

Though longer than the standard phrase, this setting still respects the primacy of the unit of four beats. (None of the Song tunes preserved in Chinese sources has a line as long as ten syllables.)

Example 12. Excerpt from Jiang Kui's third secular song (Picken 1966)

In sum, WV and SL, though comprising a very limited body of music, provide impressive confirmation for the assumptions on which Picken based his transcriptions of Song music. That such confirmation should come from sources unknown to him at the time his transcriptions were made is doubly impressive.

### III. History of the tunes in the Korean court repertoire

I have established elsewhere (Condit 1977) that, in the case of those pieces which have remained in the Korean repertoire for five hundred years or more, two evolutionary processes have been at work: metrical expansion and rhythmic equalisation. WV has undergone both of these processes, giving rise to seven separate pieces, of which six are still played today.[8] SL has undergone equalisation and is now played in a single version.

#### (a) Expanded versions of 'Walking in the Void'
The first stage in the evolution of the expanded versions of WV has already been considered above: the transformation of a tune in 4/4 so that each beat is expanded into a bar of 12/8 (Example 4). As previously noted (p. 00), the two surviving 12/8 versions (*ZTB* and *LBGM*) differ in length (*ZTB* ends with bar 44, while *LBGM* continues beyond bar 44 with a slightly varied repeat of bars 9–31). The original tune (Example 7) consisted of nine bars (beats 1–36), with a variant of the first two bars (beats 37–44) as the first line of the second verse. This

8  That the six pieces all derive from WV was established by Chang (1966).

structure may be represented graphically as follows (the numbers are beats of the original tune, bars of the expanded versions):

𝄋                                                              *fine*

1   2   3   4   5   6   7   8 9   10  11   12 etc. . . .        33  34  35  36  ‖

37  38  39  40  41  42  43  44|

*D.S.* 𝄋 *al fine*

The original tune had a total of seventy-two beats (1–44 plus repeat of 9–36), but only forty-four beats of musical material. If an expanded version were to follow the original faithfully, it would include a repeat of bars 9–36. This is true of neither *ZTB* nor *LBGM*, however. *ZTB* omits the repeat entirely and ends with bar 44; the repeat might well have been omitted because it was felt to be lacking in interest. *LBGM* repeats from bar 9, but ends five bars early, with the repeat of bar 31. The most obvious reason for omitting the last five bars of the repeat is that bar 36 would not have made a satisfactory ending (see Example 4). Since pentatonic *fa*-mode (*fa sol la do re*) was foreign to Korean ears, they would have heard WV as being in their familiar pentatonic *do*-mode (*p'yŏngjo: do re fa sol la*). Thus they would have regarded C as the final in the original tune (E♭ in the transposed expanded versions). Bar 31 was probably chosen as the ending of *LBGM*'s WV because of its emphasis on E♭.

The second stage in the evolution of the expanded versions is illustrated by the relationship between the kŏmun'go parts in *ZTB* and *SPM* Book 5 (Example 13). *SPM*-5 evidently derives

Example 13. WV, bars 9–12: *ZTB* (1572) and *SPM*-5 (*c.* 1740)

from an original of *c.* 1740 (Condit 1977: 236). It includes two versions of WV, for 'strings' and 'winds' respectively. The evolution of the 'string' version will be considered first.

Like *LBGM, SPM-5* includes the repeat from bar 9, but in *SPM-5* the first section and the repeat are in different metres. In the first section (bars 1–44), the metre has expanded from 12/8 to 20/8. In other words, the basic rhythmic unit has expanded from three quavers to five. In the two instances where *SPM-5* retains *ZTB*'s notes unchanged (boxed in the example), it can be seen that the principle underlying the metrical transformation is a doubling of the first and third quavers of *ZTB*'s three-quaver unit:

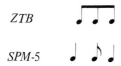

Whereas the melodic relationship between the restored fifteenth-century version and *ZTB* is quite close (Example 4), the relationship between *ZTB* and *SPM-5* is less consistent. *SPM-5* at times preserves and at times diverges from *ZTB*'s melodic outline; the most striking divergence in the example occurs in the last quarter of bar 11.

In *SPM-5*'s repeat (bars 45–71), the metre remains the same as in *ZTB* and *LBGM* (12/8), but *SPM-5* has a considerably greater number of notes per bar. *SPM-5*'s repeat follows the melodic contour of the first section quite closely, despite the differing metre.[9]

Like *LBGM, SPM-5* ends short of a complete repeat, in this case one bar early. Again, the reason for omitting the last bar is apparently that it would not have made a satisfactory ending, whereas the preceding bar, with its descent to the final (E♭), is eminently satisfactory (Example 14).

Example 14. *SPM-5*'s WV: bars 35–6 of first section and last bar of repeat

The third stage in the evolution of the expanded versions is represented by *Han's New Zither Book* (*Han kŭm sinbo*; hereafter *HNZB*), an undated kŏmun'go score. Judging from its relationship to dated scores, *HNZB* is probably from the latter half of the eighteenth century. With *HNZB*, what was originally the first section and repeat of a single piece has come to be regarded as two separate pieces. The piece corresponding to *SPM-5*'s first section is entitled simply 'WV', while the piece corresponding to *SPM-5*'s repeat is entitled: 'WV: Original *Dal Segno*'. Thus the

9  The change of metre at the repeat is not explicit in *SPM-5*'s notation. The evidence in favour of my reading of the notation will be presented on a future occasion.

direction 'dal segno' (*hwanip* in Sino-Korean) came to be used as a noun designating the repeated portion of WV. (For *HNZB* and subsequent sources, the repeated portion of WV, regarded as a separate piece, will hereafter be referred to as 'the DS'.) *HNZB*'s DS is longer than *SPM-5*'s repeat, however, Instead of ending with the repeat of bar 36 (corresponding to the end of the original tune), *HNZB*'s DS continues with a repeat of bars 37—44. In the diagram on page 000, *HNZB*'s DS starts from the *segno* (bar 9), continues through the *fine* (bar 36), and ends with bar 44. The structural relationship between the original tune and *HNZB*'s two pieces is shown in the following diagram (as in the diagram on page 000, the numbers indicate beats of the original tune, and bars of *HNZB*'s pieces):

By the eighteenth century WV had become so far removed from the original Chinese tune that it is easy to see how such structural distortions could occur. All versions of the DS subsequent to *HNZB* have this same structure.

As illustrated in Example 15a, *HNZB*'s WV is in the main identical to *SPM-5*. In contrast, *HNZB*'s DS exhibits considerable melodic divergence from *SPM-5*, while retaining the same rhythmic style (Example 15b).

Example 15. (a) *SPM-5*: first section, and *HNZB*: WV. (b) *SPM-5*: repeat, and *HNZB*: DS

In addition to the DS, *HNZB* contains two pieces which are variations on it. These are entitled 'WV: fast DS'[10] (hereafter cited as Variation I) and 'WV: melodic reduction' (hereafter Variation II). As illustrated in Example 16, in Variation I the kŏmun'go part is transposed up an octave (except where this would put the pitch above f', in which case the octave-level of the DS is retained). The transposed part is considerably closer to *SPM-5*'s repeat than *HNZB*'s 'Original DS'. In Variation II, the upper-octave part is freely transformed into a faster version with the predominant rhythm ♩ ♪ .

Example 16. *SPM-5*: repeat; *HNZB*: DS, Variation I, Variation II

Yet another variation on the DS is found in *Three Bamboos' Zither Book* (*Samjuk kŭmbo*; hereafter *TBZB*), an undated kŏmun'go score which can be assigned to the nineteenth century. This variation is entitled 'Two-string DS' ('Yangch'ŏng hwanip'), in allusion to the regular alternation, in the kŏmun'go part, of string I (an Eb drone) and a melody string (string II or III). The melody notes constitute a highly reduced form of Variation I; each bar of Variation I becomes two bars of fast 12/8 in Variation III (Example 17).

To recapitulate: By the late sixteenth century (*ZTB*), each beat of WV was expanded into a bar of 12/8. By the mid-eighteenth century (*SPM-5*), the first section of WV was transformed

Example 17. *HNZB*: Variation I; *TBZB*: Variation III ('Two-string DS')

10  The rationale behind this title is unclear. Since the DS and Variation I are identical in rhythmic style, it seems unlikely that they were performed at notably different speeds. Perhaps there is a psychological connection between higher pitch and 'fastness'.

from triple (12/8) to quintuple metre (20/8), while the repeat remained in triple metre. Sometime later in the eighteenth century (*HNZB*), the repeat came to be regarded as a separate piece,
and gave rise to two variations. A third variation was created in the nineteenth century. Thus a
single piece had become five pieces: WV (corresponding to the first section of *SPM-5*), the DS,
and three variations on the DS.

All five of these pieces remain in the current repertoire. Since *HNZB*, WV has undergone
another expansion: each quaver has expanded sixfold in the first half of the piece (bars 1–22),
becoming a dotted minim, and threefold in the second half (bars 23–44), becoming a dotted
crotchet; the quintuple metre is retained (Example 18).

In the slower first half of the piece (Example 18a), the metrical expansion is accompanied by
considerable melodic elaboration, occasionally diverging from *HNZB*'s melodic outline (for
example, in the third quarter of bar 9). Most of the changes found in the modern version had
already taken place by the time of *Yuyeji*, a kŏmun'go score from the first third of the nineteenth century. On the other hand, in the faster second half of the piece (Example 18b), *HNZB*

Example 18. WV: *HNZB* and modern performance: (a) bars 9–10; (b) bars 25–8

and modern performance exhibit the same melodic and rhythmic style, although there have been changes in melodic detail. (The two versions are transcribed with differing basic note-values – quaver and dotted crotchet – on the assumption that the tempo of *HNZB* was faster than that of modern performance. The crotchets are dotted in the transcription of modern performance because subdivisions of the beat, when they occur, are always triple, as in Example 18b, bars 26 and 27.) Since *HNZB* is in turn largely identical to *SPM*-5 (Example 15a, p. 20), it appears that the faster second half of the present-day WV has remained substantially the same since about 1740.

The DS and its variations have undergone much less change since *HNZB* and *TBZB*. No further expansion is evident, though there are differences in melodic detail (greatest in Variation I and least in Variation III) (Example 19). (Again, the different basic note-values used in the transcriptions of *HNZB* and modern performance indicate a presumed decrease in pace.)

Example 19. Bars 1–4 in *HNZB* and modern performance of (a) DS, (b) Variation I, (c) Variation II. (d) Bars 1–8 of Variation III in *TBZB* and modern performance

An interesting rule which holds true of the modern derivatives of WV is that the degree of change which a given piece has undergone is inversely proportional to pace. The fastest piece exhibits the least change (Variation III: cf. Example 19d), while the slowest piece exhibits the most extensive change (first half of WV: cf. Example 18a).

As mentioned above, *SPM-5* includes versions of WV for 'strings' and 'winds'. These are not string and wind parts for the same piece, but two different pieces for different ensembles (Condit 1977: 241); the two pieces are presumably of the same date (*c.* 1740). It is obvious through comparison of *SPM-5*'s 'wind' WV with subsequent versions of the same piece, that *SPM-5*'s mensural notation is faulty at numerous points. It can be corrected without great difficulty, however, on the basis of the subsequent versions, as well as internal parallel passages and *SPM-5*'s 'string' WV. Example 20 illustrates the relationship between the restored fifteenth-century version (Example 4) and *SPM-5*. Unlike the 'string' version, the 'wind' version is in the same key as the restored fifteenth-century version. Like 'string' WV, 'wind' WV is seventy-one bars in length; again, the first section (bars 1–44) is in quintuple metre, while the repeat (bars 45–71) is in triple metre.

Example 20. WV: corresponding excerpts from the restored fifteenth-century version and *SPM-5*'s 'wind' version (first section and repeat)

*SPM-5*'s 'wind' version is similar in idiom to its 'string' version (Example 13, p. 18). The 20/8 version was presumably derived from the fifteenth-century version by way of a 12/8 version (corresponding to *ZTB*) which has not survived in notation. Without an intervening 12/8 version, the gap between the fifteenth-century version and *SPM-5* is wide indeed, although a relationship is still discernible.

*SPM-5* is the only historical version of 'wind' WV which survives in notation (aside from the equalised version in *SPM-7*, treated below). While the first section of *SPM-5* has forty-four bars, the modern version of 'wind' WV has only fourteen and a half bars. 'Wind' WV has undergone such extensive melodic elaboration and transformation since the time of *SPM-5* that the relationship between the two versions is not immediately apparent. The presence of repeated bars in both versions, however, makes it possible to establish the relationship. In the modern version (considering only repetitions of entire bars), bar 2 is repeated in bars 7 and 14, and bar 3 is repeated in bars 6 and 15. Similarly, in *SPM-5*, bar 9 is repeated in bars 14 and 21, and bar 10 is repeated in bars 13 and 22. This suggests that the modern version derives from bars 8–22 of *SPM-5*'s version. Corroborating evidence is provided by sectional divisions: sections II and III of the modern version (bars 4–6 and 7–15 respectively) correspond to sections III and IV of *SPM-5*'s version (bars 11–13 and 14–22 respectively).[11] These relationships are summarised in the following diagram (circles and squares indicate repeated bars):

The relationship between *SPM-5* and modern performance is illustrated in Example 21. The modern version is represented by the part for p'iri (a double-reed pipe) — the leading instrument of the court orchestra — as transcribed by Kim (1968).

Again an enormous expansion, both metrical and melodic, is evident. As in the first half of the modern 'string' WV (Example 18), each quaver has expanded sixfold to become a dotted

Example 21. 'Wind' WV: corresponding excerpts from *SPM-5* and modern performance

11 I agree with Chang on the derivation of the modern sections II and III, but disagree with him on the derivation of the modern section I. Basing his study on the uncorrected reading of *SPM-5*, Chang traces the three bars of the modern section I to *SPM-5* bars 1–2a and 4–5a (a = first half of the bar) (Chang 1966: 14). It seems to me more likely that the modern version would derive from a single continuous portion of *SPM-5*, as suggested above. I admit, however, that no relationship is evident between the modern bar 1 and the corrected *SPM-5* bar 8.

Example 22. Relationship between the fifteenth-century version of WV and the sections of its modern derivatives

minim. The melodic line has undergone even more elaboration in the 'wind' version than in the 'string' version, but a clear relationship still obtains between the two evolutionary stages of the 'wind' version.

'Wind' WV is the sixth and last of the pieces in the current repertoire which derive from WV.

A final point of interest regarding the six pieces is the relationship of their sectional divisions to the restored fifteenth-century version. Each of the modern pieces is divided into seven sections, with the exception of 'wind' WV, which has only three sections. Example 22 shows the portions of the fifteenth-century version from which the modern sections derive. (The DS and Variations I–III all have the same sectional divisions, except that sections VI and VII begin at slightly different points in Variations II and III; these discrepancies will not be considered here.) Most of the surviving scores from the eighteenth century or later also indicate the same sectional divisions.

The striking feature of Example 22 is that the first four occurrences of the demisemiquaver turn on F have become section endings in the modern pieces ('string' WV, sections I–IV; 'wind' WV, sections I –III; DS and variations, sections I, II, IV). These four identical beats in the fifteenth-century version have expanded into four identical bars in each of the modern pieces, thus constituting a refrain recurring at irregular intervals. Hence, what was originally a detail of ornamentation has become a structural feature of major importance. Similarly, the two occurrences of the melodic figure C D F have become section beginnings ('string' WV, DS and variations, sections VI and VII). Again, the identical two-and-a-half-beat figure in the fifteenth-century version has become identical stretches of two and a half bars in each of the modern pieces. (It is fascinating to note that this three-note figure has evolved into identical stretches despite the difference in rhythmic position of the two occurrences (bars 7—8, beats 4-1-2; bar 10, beats 1-2-3).) In general, the six modern pieces exhibit variety of melodic and rhythmic style, but because of their common derivation from a single tune, they also share a unity of larger structural dimensions.

|  | popular title | 'elegant' title | ensemble |
|---|---|---|---|
| 'String' WV | 'Pohŏsa' 'Walking in the Void' | 'Hwanghach'ŏng' 'The Yellow River Is Clear' | plucked and struck strings |
| DS | 'Todŭri'[12] *'Dal Segno'* | 'Suyŏnjang' 'Longevity Prolonged' | full orchestra or chamber ensemble |
| Var. I | 'Ut-todŭri' 'Upper *Dal Segno*'[13] | 'Sŏngguyŏ' 'Praising with the Nine Similitudes'[14] | chamber ensemble |
| Var. II | 'Ujo karak todŭri' 'Ujo Melody *Dal Segno*'[15] | — | chamber ensemble |
| Var. III | 'Yangch'ŏng todŭri' 'Two-String *Dal Segno*' | — | chamber ensemble |
| 'Wind' WV | 'Pohŏja'[16] 'Walking in the Void' | 'Changch'un pullo' 'Everlasting Spring and Eternal Youth' | full orchestra minus plucked strings |

The modern titles and ensembles for each of the six pieces are given in the table Variations II and III are usually heard as the third and second movements respectively of a three-movement suite called 'Ch'ŏnnyŏn manse' ('A Thousand Years, a Myriad Generations'). (The first movement of this suite — 'Kyemyŏn karak todŭri' — is unrelated to WV.)

### (b) Equalised version of 'Spring in Luoyang'

Whereas WV has undergone metrical expansion, SL has undergone rhythmic equalisation. An equalised version of SL is preserved in Book 6 of *SPM*. In light of the similarity of *SPM*-6 to modern performance, we may assume that the contents of *SPM*-6 are of the same date as the compilation of the score — that is, late nineteenth-century.[17] Example 23 illustrates the relation-

12  *Todŭri* is the Korean equivalent of Sino-Korean *hwanip* (= *dal segno*).
13  'Upper' refers to the fact that the kŏmun'go part is transposed up an octave.
14  An allusion to a line from the *Book of Songs*.
15  *Ujo* here designates the mode-key of the piece: pentatonic *do*-mode in E♭ (E♭ F A♭ B♭ C).
16  The different last character in the titles *Pohŏsa* and *Pohŏja* ('string' and 'wind' WV) does not affect the meaning.
17  *SPM*-6 gives a single melody with three separate columns of plucking-indications in parallel — one column each for kŏmun'go, kayagŭm (12-stringed zither), and lute. The plucking-indications are ignored here, and the melody is transcribed in the treble clef to facilitate comparison with other versions.

*corrected from B♭ to B♮.

Example 23. SL: corresponding excerpts from *SPM*-4 (*c.* 1450) and *SPM*-6 (1892)

ship between the fifteenth-century version of SL preserved in *SPM*-4 and the nineteenth-century version in *SPM*-6.

The evolutionary process evident here is entirely different from that discussed in the preceding section. The notes of *SPM*-4's tune are retained unchanged in *SPM*-6, but the rhythm is distorted. Whereas *SPM*-4 has three different durations (crotchet, quaver, semiquaver), *SPM*-6 is limited to two durations (minim, crotchet). Furthermore, the shorter of *SPM*-6's two durations (crotchet) occurs considerably more frequently than the longer (minim). In essence, *SPM*-4's durations have been equalised, with occasional doubling of the basic duration. The doubled durations are naturally heard as phrase endings.

Example 24 illustrates the relationship between *SPM*-6 and modern performance. Two parts are given for modern performance — those played in unison respectively by the chimes and by the winds and bowed strings.

*SPM*-6's version is retained virtually unchanged in the modern chimes, but there are occasional interpolated notes in the modern winds/strings. The rule governing these interpolations is quite simple: wherever *SPM*-6 has a repeated note, the note one or two scale-steps above is interpolated between the two repetitions (Chang 1966: 140–1). In the example, d″ is interpolated between repeated c″s in bar 9; c″ between repeated g′s in bars 9–10, 11–12, 12–13; and c″ between repeated a′s in bar 11. Interpolated notes are usually 'extra' rhythmically as well as melodically; they may be either a dotted crotchet (bars 9, 10, 12, 13) or a quaver in length (bars 10, 13). Occasionally, however, they 'rob' the melody note of part of its value (as the c″ in bar 11).

The modern version is known either as 'Nagyangch'un' ('SL') or by its 'elegant' title, 'Kisu yŏngch'ang' ('Long Life and Eternal Prosperity'). The two surviving historical versions and the modern version are given in their entirety in Example 25. The transcription of *SPM*-4 follows

Example 24. SL: corresponding excerpts from *SPM*-6 and modern performance

Example 25. SL: *SPM*-4 (*c.* 1450), *SPM*-6 (1892), and modern performance

the original layout, with the first note of the repeat (a′) appearing after the varied beginning of the second verse, and with the *segno* indicating the repeat from the second beat of bar 3. As in the case of WV, the structure of SL has become distorted over the centuries. *SPM*-6 ends the piece not at the point corresponding to the end of the original tune, but with the last c′ of the varied beginning (halfway through *SPM*-4's bar 10). This point was no doubt chosen as the end because it conforms to the cadential pattern of a descent to the note an octave below the central note. (Again as with WV, Koreans would have regarded SL as being in C *do*-mode). Unlike *SPM*-4, *SPM*-6 does not notate the first note of the repeat after the varied beginning. Modern performance, on the other hand, ends with this note, as if *SPM*-4 were read straight through (with the rhythm distorted), ignoring the indication to repeat. The only discrepancy among the three versions as to notes (aside from the interpolated notes in the modern winds/bowed strings) is the omission of f′ in the antepenultimate bar of the modern version. The f′ is replaced by an interpolated g′, thus making this bar identical to bar 6. (The modern version is recorded on Lyrichord LLST 7206: *Korean Court Music*.)

### (c) Equalised expanded version of 'Walking in the Void'

The final piece to be considered is the equalised expanded version of WV, so called because the durations of an expanded version of the tune – *SPM*-5's 'wind' WV – have been equalised. The equalised version is preserved in Book 7 of *SPM*. Although *SPM*-7's WV does not survive in modern performance, its version of GPJ does survive. In light of the similarity of *SPM*-7's GPJ to modern performance (Condit 1977: 242), we may assume that *SPM*-7, like *SPM*-6, represents late-nineteenth-century performance practice. Example 26 illustrates the relationship between *SPM*-5 and *SPM*-7. Although *SPM*-7's part is labelled as being for the iron-slab chime (pang-hyang), the various instruments of the ensemble probably played virtually in unison (Condit 1977: 241).

The two versions display enough differences in sequence of notes to suggest that *SPM*-7 does not derive directly from *SPM*-5, but from a similar version (compare Example 23, in which the two versions of SL agree precisely as to notes). *SPM*-5's durations (dotted crotchet, crotchet, quaver, semiquaver) are equalised in *SPM*-7 (crotchet), with occasional doublings (minim). In this case the doublings usually occur on the last note of each of *SPM*-5's half-bars; this rule holds throughout the piece.

30

Example 26. WV: corresponding excerpts from *SPM*-5 (*c.* 1740) and *SPM*-7 (1892)

Example 27. WV: corresponding excerpts from *SPM*-5's repeat and *SPM*-7's DS

While the first section of *SPM*-7's WV is equalised, the DS remains in the same triple metre as *SPM*-5's repeat. The two versions are quite close to one another, as illustrated in Example 27. (The doubling of *SPM*-5's basic note-value in the transcription of *SPM*-7 represents a presumed slowing in the pace of performance between 1740 and 1892.)

Since *SPM*-7's version of WV does not survive in modern performance, no further stages in the evolution of the equalised expanded version can be considered.


## IV. Summary

The preceding analysis represents a journey starting from the fifteenth and sixteenth centuries, and moving both backward in time to the eleventh century and forward to the present day. On the backward journey, two Chinese tunes of the Song dynasty have been restored to their probable original forms. The tunes were seen to confirm the assumptions on which Laurence Picken based his transcriptions of the Song tunes preserved in Chinese sources. On the forward journey, we have witnessed the transformation of these simple tunes through the processes of metrical expansion and rhythmic equalisation. The expanded versions of WV have become ever more elaborate and further removed from the original, developing finally into a series of six pieces

31

with a marvellous diversity of style. The equalised versions, on the other hand, have become frozen at particular stages — the modern version of SL preserves the fifteenth-century tune, and *SPM*-7's WV preserves an eighteenth-century expanded version, both in rhythmically distorted form. The history of the two tunes is summarised in the following diagram.

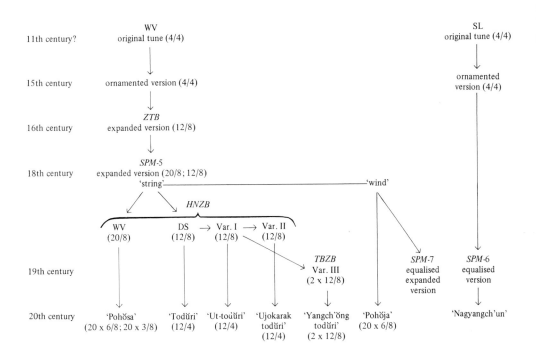

**Comparative score of 'Walking in the Void'**

In order to illustrate more fully the evolutionary processes undergone by WV, a comparative
score is presented on the following pages. The score includes fifteen versions of the tune; the
transcribed portion of each version is that deriving from bars 3 and 4 of the original tune. Versions of the first section appear in Ex. 29, versions of the corresponding part of the repeat (DS)
in Ex. 30. At the top of each of the two double-page spreads is given the hypothetical original
form of the tune. ('11th century?' appears in brackets to indicate that this form of the tune is
not preserved as such but was arrived at through analysis.) Below that, the 'string' versions
appear on the upper half of the page, the 'wind' versions on the lower half. The major evolutionary stages of the first section are represented in Ex. 29 by the restored fifteenth-century version
(preceding both 'string' and 'wind' versions; again, brackets indicate that this form of the tune
was reached through analysis), *ZTB*'s 12/8 expanded version (16th century, 'string' only),
*SPM*-5's 20/8 expanded version (18th century, 'string' and 'wind'), *SPM*-7's equalised expanded
version (19th century, 'wind' only), and the modern expanded versions (20th century, 'string'
and 'wind'). The evolutionary stages of the DS are represented in Ex. 30 by the restored
fifteenth-century version (again, preceding both 'string' and 'wind' versions), *SPM*-5's 12/8
expanded version (18th century, 'string' and 'wind'), *SPM*-7's expanded version (19th century,
'wind' only), and the modern versions of the DS and Variations I–III. All string parts are for
kŏmun'go; the historical wind parts were probably played in unison by flutes, p'iri, bowed
strings, and chimes. Each version is given in a column. To read a given version continuously,
the column is read from top to bottom; to trace the evolution of a given beat of the restored
fifteenth-century version, the double-page spread is read across from left to right. To facilitate
comparison, broken bar-lines indicate the segments of each bar deriving from a semiquaver in
the fifteenth-century version. Throughout the body of the essay, the modern versions are
transcribed, for analytical purposes, so that one bar is equivalent to one beat of the original
tune. In the comparative score, however, the barring of the modern versions follows modern
performance practice – that is, each bar corresponds to one cycle of the modern drum part.
Thus each beat of the restored fifteenth-century tune becomes two bars in modern performance, for all versions except Variation II of the DS, in which it becomes one bar. In order to
conserve space, the modern p'iri part of 'wind' WV (lower right section of Ex. 29) has been
reduced to its melodic outline: as illustrated in Example 28, each beat (dotted crotchet) is
reduced to a single note (the note of longest duration within the span of the beat). When reduced
in this way, the p'iri part becomes identical to the part for the bowed zither (ajaeng).

Example 28. Modern 'wind' WV, bar 4: p'iri part in full and reduced form

Example 29. 'Walking in the Void': excerpt from the first section

20th c.

section III

25

section IV

30

20th c.

section II

10

section III

15

Example 30. 'Walking in the Void': excerpt from the repeat

20th c.

37

## Bibliography

Chang Sa-hun 1966. *Studies in Korean music (Kugak non'go)*, Seoul
Condit, J. 1976. 'Sources for Korean music, 1450–1600', unpublished doctoral dissertation, Cambridge
Condit, J. 1977. 'The evolution of *Yŏmillak* from the fifteenth century to the present day', *Articles on Asian music: Festschrift for Dr Chang Sa-hun*, Seoul
Condit, J., in press. 'A fifteenth century Korean score in mensural notation', *Musica Asiatica* II, Oxford
Lee Hye-ku 1967. *Introduction to Korean music (Han'guk ŭmak sŏsŏl)*, Seoul
Lee Hye-ku 1972. 'A comparison of *Hyumyŏng* and *Ch'ŏngsan pyŏlgok*' (*Hyumyŏng kwa Ch'ŏngsan pyŏlgok ŭi pigyo*), *Studies in Korean music (Han'guk ŭmak yŏn'gu)* II, Seoul
Kim Ki-soo 1968. *Anthology of Korean music* I, Seoul
Marett, A.J. 1976. 'Hakuga's flute score: a tenth-century Japanese source of "Tang-music" in tablature', unpublished doctoral dissertation, Cambridge
Marett, A.J. 1977. 'Tunes notated in flute-tablature from a Japanese source of the tenth century', *Musica Asiatica* I, Oxford
Picken, L.E.R. 1957. 'Chiang K'uei's nine songs for Yueh', *The Musical Quarterly* XLIII no. 2
Picken, L.E.R. 1966. 'Secular Chinese songs of the twelfth century', *Studia Musicologica Academiae Scientiarum Hungaricae* VIII, Budapest
Picken, L.E.R. 1967. 'Central Asian tunes in the Gagaku tradition', *Festschrift Walter Wiora*, Kassel
Picken, L.E.R. 1969a. 'Music and musical sources of the Sonq dynasty', *Journal of the American Oriental Society* LXXXIX no. 3
Picken, L.E.R. 1969b. 'Tunes apt for T'ang lyrics from the shō part-books of Tōgaku', *Essays in Ethnomusicology: A Birthday Offering for Lee Hye-ku*, Seoul
Picken, L.E.R. 1971a. 'A twelfth-century secular Chinese song in zither tablature', *Asia Major* XVI parts 1–2
Picken, L.E.R. 1971b. 'Some Chinese terms for musical repeats, sections, and forms, common to T'ang Yüan, and Tōgaku scores', *Bulletin of the School of Oriental and African Studies* XXXIV part 1
Picken, L.E.R. 1973. ' "The waves of Kokonor": a dance tune of the T'ang dynasty', *Asian Music* V part 1 (with Rembrandt Wolpert, Allan Marett, and Jonathan Condit)
Picken, L.E.R., in press. 'Mouth organ and lute parts of Tōgaku and their interrelationships', *Musica Asiatica* III, Oxford (with R.F. Wolpert)
Wolpert, R.F. 1975. 'Lute music and tablatures of the T'ang period', unpublished doctoral dissertation, Cambridge

**Glossary**

ajaeng 牙箏
Changch'un pullo 長春不老
Ch'ŏnnyon manse 千年萬歲
ci 詞
Han kŭm sinbo 韓琴新譜
Hwanghach'ŏng 黃河清
hwanip 還入
hyangak 鄉樂
Jiang Kui 姜夔
jueju 絕句
Kisu yŏngch'ang 其壽永昌
Koryŏ-sa 高麗史
Kŭm hapcha-bo 琴合字譜
ling 令
Nagyangch'un 洛陽春
Ouyang Xiu 歐陽修
panghyang 方響
Pohŏja 步虛子
Pohŏsa 步虛詞
p'yŏngjo 平調
Samjuk kŭmbo 三竹琴譜
Sejong sillok 世宗實錄
Sinjŭng kŭmbo 新證琴譜
Sogak wŏnbo 俗樂源譜
Songguyŏ 頌九如
Suyŏnjang 壽延長
Tangak 唐樂
Taeak hubo 大樂後譜
Yangch'ŏng hwanip 雨清還入
Yi (dynasty) 李
Yŏmillak 與民樂
Yuyeji 遊藝志

# 'Banshiki Sangun' and 'Shōenraku': metrical structure and notation of two Tang-music melodies for flute

ALLAN MARETT

## I. Introduction

The flute score *Hakuga fue-fu* was compiled in A.D. 966 from a number of earlier source-scores by the courtier—musician Minamoto no Hiromasa, also known as Hakuga (918—80). Rather than reflecting a style of performance current in Hakuga's own time, the score appears to record an earlier performance tradition that had almost, or totally, died out by the middle of the tenth century. When Hakuga wrote (in a postface to the score) that in order to record a dying tradition he had copied pieces from a number of earlier sources in their original notational style, it appears that he was not indulging in purely conventional (and thus rather meaningless) lament for a glorious and lost tradition, as some commentators suggest (Harich-Schneider 1973: 194), but was stating a truth about the tradition he had recorded. Several observations support this view. First, a comparison of pieces that occur both in *Hakuga fue-fu* and in later manuscripts from the Tōgaku tradition of Japanese court music (for example the eleventh-century (?) source *Kaichū-fu*, or the fourteenth-century source *Chū Ōga ryūteki yōroku-fu*) shows not only that the notational methods differ (particularly with regard to mensuration), but also that the melodies yielded by the later notations, while recognisably the same as those in *Hakuga fue-fu*, are more highly ornamented, and reflect a different style of performance. Secondly, six different

41

notational styles may be distinguished in *Hakuga fue-fu* (Marett 1978a); this supports Hakuga's statement that pieces from a number of source-scores of earlier date were copied preserving the original notational styles. Two styles (Systems I and II) used in a majority of pieces have been dealt with in a previous paper (Marett 1977). The two pieces to be considered here, 'Banshiki Sangun', a suite in twenty-three sections, and 'Shōenraku', a short piece in one movement, are in a third, probably older, notation. It is possible that both pieces had been dropped from the repertory by the end of the ninth century: neither piece occurs in any source other than *Hakuga fue-fu*.

This paper offers transcriptions of 'Banshiki Sangun' and 'Shōenraku', together with an explanation of the principles of decipherment. Not only are the resulting melodies strikingly attractive: from a metrical point of view, 'Banshiki Sangun' is perhaps the most interesting of all Tōgaku tunes.

*Hakuga fue-fu* exists in late copies only. The main source for this study was a copy of a copy made in 1731 by Toyohara no Tomoaki. This copy — now held in the Rakusaidō collection of the Research Archives for Japanese Music, Ueno Gakuen College, Tokyo — is one of the earliest and most reliable surviving copies. A second copy — held in the Tokyo University of the Arts (catalogue number 1363 16.15.1.1) — is also cited. The very late date of the copies (in relation to the original) should be noted; as might be expected, copyists' errors are many.

## II. Tablature signs and pitch

A full account of the relationship between tablature signs, mode and pitch in *Hakuga fue-fu* has been given elsewhere (Marett 1977: 3–9). A brief summary of the relationship between tablature signs and pitch in the Banshiki mode (the mode of 'Banshiki Sangun') and in the Ōshiki mode (the mode of 'Shōenraku') is given below.

It has been suggested that during the Heian period (A.D. 794–1185) and perhaps even as late as the thirteenth century, the Banshiki and Ōshiki modes were the same as the correspondingly named modes in the Chinese system of the Tang dynasty (618–907) (Marett 1977: 9). In the Tang system, the Ōshiki mode was a Dorian on A: A B C D E F♯ G; the Banshiki mode, a Dorian on B: B C♯ D E F♯ G♯ A.

In order to realise these modes correctly, a performer must produce the following pitches with successive fingerings, indicated by tablature signs (Marett 1977: 3) in *Hakuga fue-fu*.

| Ōshiki mode: | 六 | 丁 | 中 | 夕 | 上 | 五 | 干 |
|---|---|---|---|---|---|---|---|
| | D | C | B | A | G | F♯ | E |
| Banshiki mode: | 六 | 丁 | 中 | 夕 | 上 | 五 | 干 |
| | D | C♯ | B | A | G♯ | F♯ | E |

These pitch-values for tablature-signs have been adopted in transcribing 'Banshiki Sangun' and 'Shōenraku'. Note that 丁 implies C♮ in the Ōshiki mode, but C♯ in the Banshiki mode; 上 implies G♮ in the Ōshiki mode, but G♯ in the Banshiki mode; 口 (the fingering with

Figure 1. Notation of 'Shōenraku' from *Hakuga fue-fu*

all fingerholes closed; Marett 1977: 4) in Heian times yielded D, rather than C♯ as it does on the present-day ryūteki (flute). The structure of the Banshiki mode in the Heian period was different from that which it has today. It is not known how G♯ (not used in present-day Tōgaku) was obtained on the ryūteki in the Heian period; in modern performance of Saibara (a Gagaku genre) this pitch is obtained by half-covering the ⊥ hole.

## III. Rhythm and metre in 'Shōenraku'

Since the metrical structure of 'Banshiki Sangun' is complex, we shall first consider the mensural notation of 'Shōenraku', an example considerably simpler than 'Banshiki Sangun'.

Figure 1 is the notation of 'Shōenraku' (reproduced from the copy of *Hakuga fue-fu* in the Tokyo University of the Arts (see above)). Immediately following the title is written: 'there are ten *hyōshi*'. Picken (1966: 131) has shown that in China of the Song dynasty (960–1280) the term *pai* (*zi*)/*hyō* (*shi*) had two meanings: 'beat' and 'measure'. In the present context the meaning of 'hyōshi' is almost certainly 'measure'; we may therefore translate the passage as 'there are ten *measures*'. It is unlikely that at the time of Hakuga, 'hyōshi' had the meaning that it has today, 'a sequence of four (or eight) measures' (see further, pp. 54–6).

In almost all measured pieces in *Hakuga fue-fu* there is only one stroke per measure on the large drum, taiko (notated by the sign 百 ). It might therefore be expected that, in the present case, the number of measures (hyōshi) and the number of taiko-strokes will be the same, namely ten. In Figure 1, however, only eight taiko-strokes are notated; two 百 appear to have been omitted (see below).

In making a preliminary reading of Figure 1, the following mensural values have been attributed to signs (Marett 1977: 12–22):

1. Each unqualified tablature sign ( 六 丁 中 夕 上 五 干 ) represents a note of one beat in duration.

2. The sign 二 repeats the preceding tablature sign and, unless otherwise qualified, has a value of one beat.

3. The sign リ (a cursive form of the character 引 ) prolongs the value of the preceding note by one beat (two beats in all). In the 'Notes on the method of scoring' (*Ampu-hō*) appended to *Hakuga fue-fu*, リ is defined as 'lengthen by long blowing'.

The total number of beats yielded by application of these values is 87. 百 signs (that is, taiko-strokes) do not occur, as they do in most pieces in the Tōgaku tradition, at regular intervals; here they occur as follows (numbers indicate beats):

5 百 10 百 9 百 8 百 10 百 9 百 8 百 26 百 2

In order to regularise the sequence of drum-strokes the interpretation of the sign リ requires further qualification as follows:

リ prolongs the preceding note by one beat if, and only if, the preceding note occurs on beat 1, 3, 5, or 7 of a measure; if the preceding note falls on beat 2, 4, 6, or 8, it is not to be prolonged.

When this modification is adopted in reading the notation of 'Shōenraku', taiko-strokes fall at the following intervals:

4 百 8 百 8 百 8 百 8 百 8 百 8 百 24 百 2

and the sequence of drum-strokes is for the most part regular.

Example 1. 'Shōenraku'

The regularity of this metrical structure suggests that the values postulated for signs are correct. If the two omitted 百 signs (see above) are restored between the seventh and eighth written 百, the following metrical structure emerges:

4 百 8 百 8 百 8 百 8 百 8 百 8 百 8 (百) 8 (百) 8 百 2

Two beats missing after the final 百 are due to the failure of a copyist to duplicate the final minim a' (see Example 1: on the conventions employed in transcription, see p. 56 below).

Parallels between the mensural notation of 'Shōenraku' and the mensural notation used in the majority of pieces in *Hakuga fue-fu* (Systems I and II) (see above) support the interpretation of signs in 'Shōenraku' offered above.

Pieces in System I and System II yield regular metrical structures if, and only if, the following values are attributed to signs (Marett 1977: 12–22):

1. Each unqualified tablature sign represents a note of one beat in duration (as in 'Shōenraku').
2. The sign 二 repeats the preceding tablature-sign and, unless otherwise qualified, has a value of one beat (as in 'Shōenraku').
3. The sign 火 (not present in 'Shōenraku'), defined in 'Notes on the method of scoring' as 'very quick', indicates, in most instances, that the signs before and after it represent half a beat (transcribed ♪ ).
4. The sign ⌒ (not present in 'Shōenraku') indicates prolongation of the preceding note if, and only if, it follows beats 1, 3, 5, or 7. After beats 2, 4, 6, or 8, ⌒ (defined as 'interrupt the breath') indicates that a breath is to be taken.
5. A note followed by リ is prolonged by one beat; when リ is followed on beats 2 or 6 of any measure by ⌒ (thus リ ⌒), it is to be prolonged to four beats.

As a demonstration of this mensural notation in action, a transcription of 'Hakuchū' (System I), together with the original tablature, is given below in Example 2. Each measure is eight beats in length, with the taiko-stroke on beat 5. Notes prolonged by ⌒ (see 4) are transcribed ♩ ♩ in order to differentiate them from notes prolonged by リ , transcribed ♩. After beats 2, 4, 6, and 8, ⌒ (transcribed vertically ǀ ) marks points at which a breath is to be taken. リ ⌒ is transcribed ♩ ♩.

Example 2. 'Hakuchū' (Marett 1977)

The function of ⌐ in Systems I and II, as a sign that indicates prolongation after beats 1, 3, 5, or 7 but not after beats 2, 4, 6, or 8, is clearly the same as the function of 〵 in 'Shōenraku'. It will be shown below that the principle whereby a prolongation sign ( ⌐ in Systems I and II; 〵 in 'Shōenraku') functions only after beats 1, 3, 5, or 7 holds true not only for the thirty or so pieces in Systems I and II, and 'Shōenraku', but also for 'Banshiki Sangun'.

### IV. Rhythm and metre in 'Banshiki Sangun'

'Banshiki Sangun' is a suite in two movements, each comprising a number of sections (*jō*) as follows: first movement (Prelude (*Jo*)), thirteen sections (numbered I–XIII); second movement (Broaching (*Ha*)), ten sections (numbered I–X); in all, twenty-three sections. As stated above, the metrical structure of 'Banshiki Sangun' is complex. Differing metres may be observed in different sections of each movement, and even within a single section. For this reason, the notation of 'Banshiki Sangun' will be considered under a number of headings.

#### (a) Prelude, Sections IV to XII

Each section (IV–XII) comprises twelve measures, but in some sections the final measure (measure 12) is in a different metre from the preceding measures. In the sections under discussion, the notation of measures 1–11 yields regular 8/4 measures with the taiko-stroke on beat 5 if, and only if, the notation is read in the same way as that of 'Shōenraku' (see Example 4 below). In addition to the signs already encountered in 'Shōenraku', 'Banshiki Sangun' exhibits the sign 火 . As in Systems I and II (see above), 火 halves the duration of the signs before and after it.

The final measure (measure 12) of each section is not so easily read, however: Table 1 shows the notation of this measure in each section (IV–XII).

Table 1. *The notation of measure 12 in Sections IV–XII*

| Section | Notation |
|---------|----------|
| IV | 五 六 丁 中 百 |
| V | 五 六 丁 中 百 〵 中 丁 中 〵 |
| VI | 五 六 丁 中 百 〵 中 丁 中 〵 |
| VII | 五 六 丁 中 百 〵 中 丁 中 〵 |
| VIII | 五 六 丁 中 百 〵 中 丁 中 |
| IX | 五 六 丁 中 百 中 二 〵 |
| X | 五 六 丁 中 百 〵 |
| XI | 五 六 丁 中 百 〵 |
| XII | 五 六 丁 中 百 |

(a) Excluding from consideration Sections IV and IX (see below), it appears that measure 12 was the same in Sections V–XII and consisted of ten beats with 百 on beat 5. Subsequently errors occurred in Sections VIII–XII. Sections V–VII have a final measure of the ten-beat form. In Sections VIII–XII, however, the number of beats declines with each successive section, in a way that suggests an accumulation of copyists' errors as each section was copied from the preceding section (see Table 1): in Section VIII, the final sign 刂 is omitted; in Sections X and XI, the last four signs 中 丁 中 刂 are omitted; in Section XII the last five signs 刂 中 丁 中 刂 appear to be omitted (but see (d) below). A ten-beat final measure such as this (in effect, a metrical cadence – see below) is to be found in no other piece in the Tōgaku tradition.

(b) At first sight, the final five beats of Section IV appear also to have been omitted; closer investigation suggests, however, that the occurrence of a final measure of five beats may not be an error. Measure 1 of the following section (V) includes seven rather than the usual four beats before the 百 (taiko-stroke) sign. If the first three beats in Section V are allowed to occupy the final three (missing) beats of Section IV, measure 12 (making eight beats in both Section IV, measure 12, and Section V, measure 1), the regular succession of 8/4 measures is undisturbed (see Example 4). Although Section IV differs from the sections previously considered, in that its final measure is eight rather than ten beats in length, the instruction 'play slowly both times' at the end of Section V suggests that Sections IV and V together should be considered as a pair of metrically regular movements; an interruption of the regular metre by the insertion of a cadential ten-beat measure might well be felt to be inappropriate.

(c) In Section IX, measure 12 differs melodically from measure 12 in other sections; as in Section IV, it is eight beats in length.

(d) Another instance of a metrically unbroken succession of sections occurs between Section XII and Section XIII; the apparent omission of the signs 刂 中 丁 中 刂 in Section XII, measure 12 (see (a) above) is therefore probably not an error, as earlier suggested, except in the case of the first 刂 (see Example 4). Section XIII, like Section V, contains more than four beats (namely six) before the taiko-stroke ( 百 ) in measure 1. If the first two of these six beats are allowed to occupy the final empty beats of Section XII bar 12, the metrical structure is exactly parallel to that of Sections IV and V.

The psychological effect of final measures of ten beats is one of finality – a metrical cadence. By way of contrast, Section IV continues directly into Section V, Section IX continues directly into Section X, and Section XII continues directly into Section XIII (see Example 4). This metrical contrast is but one of several unusual metrical features in this suite (see further pp. 53–4).

The mensural notation of both 'Shōenraku' and 'Banshiki Sangun' (Prelude, Sections IV to XII including the twelfth measure in each) may be summarised as follows:

1. Each unqualified tablature sign represents one beat.
2. The sign 二 indicates that a note is to be repeated.
3. The sign 刂 implies prolongation by one beat where it follows an odd-numbered beat (1, 3, 5, 7); but where it follows an even-numbered beat, it does not imply prolongation.
4. The sign 火 halves the duration of the preceding and succeeding signs.

### (b) Prelude, Sections I to III

In making a preliminary transcription of Sections I–III of Prelude (*Jo*) (see Example 3), the metrical values adopted for the *preliminary* analysis of 'Shōenraku' (see above) have been adopted, namely: (a) each unqualified tablature sign represents a note of one beat in duration; (b) the sign 二 repeats the preceding tablature sign, and, unless otherwise qualified, has a value of one beat; (c) the sign リ prolongs the value of the preceding note by one beat ( リ does not have the value proposed for Prelude, Sections IV–XII – see further, p. 00). When signs are read in this way, the total number of beats yielded in each section is: Section I, 150 beats; Section II, 147 beats; Section III, 144 beats. It is clear from the instruction that precedes the notations under discussion – namely 'Prelude, thirteen sections, each of twelve measures' – that each section comprises twelve measures. The average number of beats per measure has therefore been calculated by dividing the total number of beats in each section by the number of measures (12): Section I, 12½ beats per measure (150 divided by 12); Section II, 12¼ beats per measure (147 divided by 12); Section III, 12 beats per measure (144 divided by 12). These results suggest that each measure should consist of twelve beats; extra beats are probably due to copyists' errors. (Measures 11 and 12 of Section III are not in fact twelve beats in length, as will be shown below.)

The view that measures consist of twelve beats is further confirmed by analysis of the melodic structure, and the relationship of the melodic structure to the placing of taiko-stroke signs ( 百 ). Before taking up this matter, however, it is necessary to consider an unusual method of notating taiko-strokes in the sections under discussion.

The total absence of 百 signs in Section I suggests that the taiko was silent in this section. ( 百 is similarly absent from the older-style notations of two other pieces in *Hakuga fue-fu*, namely: 'Moto-uta' and 'Bonryūshū no Jo'.)

In Section II, 百 signs occur not only to the right of the tablature signs, written in red ink (the usual practice in *Hakuga fue-fu*), but also (in conjunction with the red 百 ) *within* the column of tablature signs, written in black ink, thus:

> black 中 百 red
> black 百

In the absence of any explanation by Hakuga, any interpretation of this practice is speculative. Let us, however, consider the possibility that intracolumnary (black) 百 represent an archaic notational practice, and that extracolumnary (red) 百 are an editorial gloss made by Hakuga in order to make clear, to readers of his own and later times, that black intracolumnary 百 represent a taiko-stroke on the preceding (rather than the succeeding) tablature sign. Evidence in support of the view that the use of intracolumnary 百 *alone* was a valid notational practice is provided by the use in the tenth-century source *Kosō-fu* (Tenri University Library, catalogue number 761.179 jū 39; *Kogakusho ishu*: 1–54) of black intracolumnary 百 without red extracolumnary 百 . Furthermore, Hakuga makes clear in a postface to *Hakuga fue-fu* that in copying older notations he added glosses: 'For this score, however, I have adopted the tablature style of those (ancient) times. I have also added glosses.' Indeed, many examples of the editorial hand at work may be detected in the score (Marett 1976).

Example 3. Preliminary transcription of 'Banshiki Sangun', Prelude, Sections I–III

In Section II, thirteen (rather than twelve) pairs of intra- and extracolumnary 百 are notated; the third of these pairs may be disregarded as a copyist's error (see Example 4).

In Section III, five pairs of intracolumnary and extracolumnary 百 are followed by six single, extracolumnary (red) 百 : a total of eleven points at which taiko-strokes are notated. The ninth 百 has been omitted. It is possible that the omission of intracolumnary (black) 百 in Section III, after the first five, may be due to Hakuga's having abandoned the more archaic notation in favour of his own.

Having discussed the notation of taiko-strokes, we can now consider their relation to the melodic structure. A short repeated-note figure, in the rhythm ♩ 𝅗𝅥 , occurs at regular intervals throughout Sections I–III (see Example 3). The lengths of melodic phrases that end with this figure are listed below for each section.

Section I: 7, 6, 6, 7, 11, 6, 6, 5, 6, 6, 7, 15, 6, 13, 6, 6, 7 beats
Section II: 6, 6, 6, 8, 11, 6, 7, 6, 6, 6, 6, 8, 6, 6, 7, 15, 6, 8, 6, 6, 5 beats
Section III: 6, 6, 6, 6, 6, 6, 6, 7, 11, 6, 6, 6, 6, 6, 7, 6, 6, 6, 3, 25 beats

The number of occurrences of phrases of each length is:

6-beat phrases: thirty-eight occurrences
7-beat phrases: nine occurrences
11-beat phrases: four occurrences
8-beat phrases: three occurrences
3-, 5-, 10-, 13-, 15-, 25-beat phrases: one or two occurrences each

In a majority of instances, therefore, the figure ♩ ♩ marks the end of a phrase six beats in length. Phrases of 5, 7, 8, 11, and 13 beats probably derive from six-beat phrases, or multiples thereof, the notation of which has been corrupted by errors.

If measures in Prelude, Sections I–III are twelve beats in length, as was suggested above, we might expect the taiko-stroke to fall (as in most measured pieces in *Hakuga fue-fu*) at the beginning of the second half of each bar, that is, on beat 7. The half-bar, at the beginning of which the taiko-stroke falls, will then be six beats in length.

In Section II, ten out of the twelve correctly placed pairs of 百 (excluding the erroneous third pair) fall on the first beat of a phrase ending ♩ ♩. Seven of the phrases are of six beats; three, of seven beats. If it is accepted that the three seven-beat phrases are actually six-beat phrases wrongly notated, it may be concluded that in ten out of twelve measures in Section II the taiko-stroke falls on the first beat of a stereotyped phrase (that is, one ending ♩ ♩) six beats in length; and that, as postulated above, the second half-bar (from the taiko-stroke onwards) contains six beats. Furthermore, in ten out of twelve instances in Section II, the first (like the second) half of each measure is occupied by a six-beat phrase ending in ♩ ♩. In view of this, we may conclude that not only the metre of Section II but also that of Sections I and III is for the most part 12/4, as suggested earlier, with the taiko-stroke on beat 7.

In the edited transcription of Sections I–III in Example 4 (pp. 57–64), each measure (excluding measures 11, 12 of Section III – see below) has twelve beats except where the notation is hopelessly corrupt. In making this transcription, it was noticed that in the small number of instances (six in all) where ♪ follows beats 2 or 8 it appears not to have a prolongation function. With so small a sample, it is uncertain whether ♪ loses its prolongation function after *all* even-numbered beats, as in Sections IV–XII.

Finally, let us consider measures 11 and 12 of Section III, which are in a different metre from all other measures in Sections I–III. These measures anticipate the metre (8/4 + 10/4), melody, and mensural notation of corresponding measures (11 and 12) from following sections (V–VIII, X, XI – see above and Example 4). Signs clearly have the same mensural values as in Sections IV–XII (see above).

Anticipation of this sort, where metrical, melodic, and notational features appear in part of a preceding section before they are adopted fully, may also be observed in Prelude, Section XIII (see below), where the metre (6/4), notational conventions, and certain melodic features of the following sections (Broaching, Sections I–IV) are adopted in measures 8–12 (see Example 4).

### (c) Prelude, Section XIII

If Section XIII is read in the same way as the preceding nine sections (IV–XII: see pp. 46–7 above), the first four measures are, as expected, in 8/4 metre; but when the remaining eight measures (5–12) are read in this way, the resulting metre is irregular.

Regular metre reappears, however, if a different convention regarding the interpretation of the sign ⌐) is adopted for these measures, namely that the prolongation function of ⌐) is suspended after beats 3 and 6 (rather than after beats 2, 4, 6, and 8, as in Sections IV–XII). The 6/4 metre (3 + 3 beats with taiko-stroke on beat 4) that results from such a reading is that of the sections (Broaching I–IV) that succeed Prelude, Section XIII (see later).

The treatment of ⌐) in 6/4 is consistent in principle with its treatment in 8/4. In 8/4, ⌐) does not prolong after the binary units, two, four, six, and eight beats. In the compound duple metre, 6/4, it does not prolong after ternary units of three or six beats. A summary of the metrical function of all signs in 6/4 metre is given in the next section.

### (d) Broaching, Sections I to IV

Many of the ten sections of Broaching share melodic material (see Example 4). Sections I, II and IV are the same except for short two-bar incipits; Section X is the same as Section IV, save that in Section X a coda replaces the final four bars of Section IV; all sections, except Section X, have the same final four bars. By comparing passages of identical melodic material, many copyists' errors may be detected and eliminated.

When the following values (adopted in reading Prelude, Section XIII, bars 5–12 (see (c) above)) are adopted in reading Broaching, Sections I–IV, each section consists of twelve bars of 6/4 metre, with the taiko-stroke on beat 4 (see Example 4): (a) each unqualified tablature sign represents a note of one beat in duration; (b) the sign ⌐ repeats the preceding sign and, unless otherwise qualified, has a value of one beat; (c) the sign ⼃ indicates that the notes before and after it have a value of half a beat; (d) a note followed by ⌐) is prolonged for one beat, except where ⌐) follows beats 3 and 6, when it has no metrical value.

In Sections I and II (see Example 4), the first measure lacks a first beat. Although such a rhythmical feature is rare in Tōgaku, it should not (in view of the unusual rhythmical and metrical features of this suite) be dismissed as the result of copyist's error.

### (e) Broaching, Sections V to IX

Sections VIII and IX are not notated. In their place is the following instruction: 'In place of Section VIII, repeat Section VI; in place of Section IX, repeat Section VII.' In spite of some differences in their notations, Sections V and VII appear to be melodically the same; differences in detail appear to be the result of copyists' errors in Section VII, and they have been eliminated by reference to Section V (see Example 4).

The final four bars of the three notated sections, V, VI, and VII, are the same as the four final measures of Sections I–IV – that is, they are in 6/4 (see above). In Sections V and VII, however, measures 1–8 are not in 6/4 but in 4/4, with the taiko-stroke on beat 3. In the notation of these measures, as in other examples of binary metre (8/4) already encountered (Prelude IV–XII – see pp. 46–7), ♩ does not prolong after beats 2 and 4. Section VI, like Sections V and VII, includes both 4/4 and 6/4 measures; in this movement, however, the change from 4/4 to 6/4 occurs in measure 6 rather than in measure 9 (see Example 4).

### (f) Broaching, Section X

For the first eight measures Section X is the same as Section IV, and again uses the notation appropriate for 6/4 metre. In the notation of measures 9–12, there appears to be a lacuna between the fourth and fifth tablature signs. If three tablature signs and one ♩ are supplied, these measures are in 4/4 metre, notated as in Sections V–VII (see Example 4).

## V. Metre in 'Banshiki Sangun': general observations

The metrical structure (and the mensural notation) of the suite 'Banshiki Sangun' is more rich and complex than that of any other piece in *Hakuga fue-fu*, or indeed any other piece in the known Tōgaku repertory. The following features are to be noted:

(1) Five different metres are used – 12/4, 10/4, 8/4, 6/4 and 4/4. In general the metres of greater bar-lengths are used early in the suite; those of shorter bar-lengths are used later.

(2) Three different mensural notations, each involving a different function for ♩ , are used:

(a) In 12/4 metre, ♩ prolongs the preceding note by one beat. In a few instances, following beats 2 and 8, ♩ appears to have no prolongation function; these are, however, insufficient to constitute clear evidence of notational practice.

(b) In 8/4 and 4/4, ♩ prolongs the preceding note for one beat if, and only if, the note falls on beat 1, 3, 5, or 7; if the preceding note occurs on beat 2, 4, 6, or 8, ♩ does not imply prolongation. The notation thus reflects the binary nature of the metre.

(c) In 6/4, ♩ prolongs the preceding note if, and only if, the note falls on beat 1, 2, 4, or 5; if the preceding note falls on beat 3 or 6, ♩ does not imply prolongation. The notation thus reflects the ternary nature of the metre.

(3) In two instances, the introduction of a new metre and metrical notation is anticipated at the end of a preceding section: in Prelude, Section III, measures 11 and 12 anticipate the 8/4 and 10/4 metre adopted in measures 11 and 12 of many sections of the following group (IV–XIII); in Prelude, Section XIII, measures 5–12 anticipate the 6/4 metre of measures 5–12 of the following sections (Broaching, Sections I–IX).

(4) In Prelude, Sections V–VIII, X, XI, the final measure is extended from eight beats to ten, as a rhythmic cadence. In contrast, Sections IV, IX, and XII have no such cadence and continue uninterrupted in 8/4.

(5) In Broaching, Sections V–X, passages in 6/4 are juxtaposed with passages in 4/4. Two

technical terms, apparently of metrical significance, follow Sections V and VI respectively, namely: *xucuipai/kyosaihyō*, 'the *xucui/kyosai* metre' (*pai/hyō* in this context means 'metre'), and *cuipai/saihyō*, '*cui/sai* metre'.

The term *xucui/kyosai* that follows Section V is also to be found in the late Tang text *Yuefu zalu / Gakufu zatsuroku*. Here it is defined as the name of a type of movement from the Po/Ha group of movements in the Tang-Chinese 'Long Suite' (*Daqu/Taikyoku*) form (Gimm 1966: 224–31). Since Sections VII and IX are both repetitions of Section V, it might be concluded that all three movements are examples of the xucui/kyosai form. It seems probable that the xucui*pai*/kyosai*hyō*, that is the xucui/kyosai *metre*, is that exhibited by these movements, namely eight measures of 4/4 followed by four measures of 6/4; and that this metre typifies the Tang xucui/kyosai form.

The term *cui/sai* that follows Section VI also appears in *Yuefu zalu / Gakufu zatsuroku* and is likewise defined as the name of a type of movement from the *Po/Ha* of the Tang Daqu/Taikyoku. This movement-type is also known as *shicui/jissai* (Gimm 1966: 224–31). It might be concluded that Section VI together with Section VIII is an example of the shicui/jissai form, and that the overall metrical structure (five measures of 4/4 followed by seven measures of 6/4) typifies this type of movement, and is thus known as shicui*pai*/jissai*hyō* (= cui*pai*/sai*hyō*) or cui/sai *metre*.

(6) Finally, it should be noted that the metrical notation observed in 'Shōenraku' and 'Banshiki Sangun', Prelude, Sections IV–XII, where ⅃ functions as prolongation sign except after beats 2, 4, 6, and 8, is also to be observed in other pieces in *Hakuga fue-fu*, namely, 'Tokubanji (Section II)' and 'Taizoku-kaku-banshiki-chō Choka-Manzairaku'. In other aspects of their notation, however, these pieces differ slightly from 'Shōenraku' and 'Banshiki Sangun', and thus represent another system of notation.


## VI. Tempo and melodic structure

The suggestion that early Tōgaku scores should be read giving to each unqualified tablature sign the value of one beat, rather than of one measure, was first made by Picken in 1956. Indeed, an impartial reading of any such score strongly suggests that the unqualified tablature sign represents the basic metrical unit. Since a basic metrical unit is by definition a beat, not a measure (a measure is a grouping of beats), in this paper tablature signs have been regarded as beats, and transcribed as crotchets.

The practice in recent transcriptions of Tōgaku (see Shiba 1972; Garfias 1975) of notating each metrical unit (kobyōshi) not as a beat but as a four-beat measure appears to have arisen for two reasons: first, because at present-day tempos, the succession of kobyōshi (which correspond to unqualified tablature signs in *Hakuga fue-fu*) proceeds so slowly that they may not be perceived as beats; secondly, because the decorative figurations of ryūteki (flute), hichiriki (reed-pipe), and gakusō (zither) may be notated more precisely and with greater clarity within the compass of a measure than within the compass of a beat. There is, however, no evidence that at the time of Hakuga, Tōgaku pieces were played at a tempo at which kobyōshi metrical units ceased to be audible as beats. Furthermore, the decorative figurations — indeed, many of the most distinctive melodic features of the present-day ryūteki line — are not present in *Hakuga fue-fu*. We may conclude that when ancient musical documents are interpreted in terms of themselves and evidence contemporary with them, without reference to present-day interpretation, the meanings for signs that emerge differ considerably from the present-day meanings.

The melodies that emerge from reading each unmodified tablature sign as one beat also differ considerably from those carried by ryūteki and hichiriki in modern Tōgaku performance. In pieces in the current repertory, this ancient Heian melody, slowed down several times, appears as a melodic structure (no longer perceivable as a melody) carried principally by shō (mouth-organ) — in most cases, it occurs as the lowest note of each cluster chord (*aitake*) — and biwa (lute). Picken (1967: 545–51) has suggested that there is an analogy between the function of the ancient melody as a structural element in modern Tōgaku, and the function of a melody such as 'L'homme armé' (also slowed down several times) as a cantus firmus in a mediaeval mass. (This is not to imply that the structural use of old melodies in Tōgaku is a conscious compositional device, as in the cantus-firmus mass.) Picken also showed (*ibid.*) that the ancient melodies in some instances exhibit traits (also displayed by Hungarian and Cheremis folksong) similar to those identified by Szabolesi (1935) as typical of tunes of ancient Central Asia (the provenance of many Tōgaku pieces). Furthermore, Picken has shown (1969) that the ancient melodies are in many instances suitable (by the criteria of Chinese musical theory) for setting Chinese lyrics of the Tang dynasty.

In a recent paper, Condit (1976) demonstrated that when the early Tōgaku score *Jinchi-yōroku* is read in accordance with instructions given in the 'Notes on the method of scoring (*Ampu-hō*)' of that score, the melodies that emerge are similar to those of *Hakuga fue-fu*, rather than to the stylized *shizugaki* and *hayagaki* patterns of modern Tōgaku performances.

Evidence from *Hakuga fue-fu*, and in particular 'Banshiki Sangun', further confirms these views. First, let us consider how the melodies of 'Banshiki Sangun' and 'Shōenraku' would emerge from reading each unmodified tablature sign as one *measure* (whilst realising only written signs, and adding no unwritten modifications culled from modern Tōgaku performance-practice). The melody yielded by such a reading would be a slow succession of four-beat notes, broken only occasionally by an eight-beat note, and rarely by a pair of two-beat notes. The melodic line would exhibit no ornamentation (the sign 由 リ リ リ (mordent) and 由 (delayed mordent), present in some pieces in *Hakuga fue-fu*, are absent from 'Banshiki Sangun' or 'Shōenraku'). Not only does a line such as this lack melodic interest, but the rich metrical contrasts, one of the most distinctive features of 'Banshiki Sangun', are lost to the ear.

Secondly, terms such as 'xucuipai/kyosaihyō' ('empty, hurrying beats') and '(shi)cuipai/(jis)saihyō' ('(full) hurrying beats') (see above) in themselves suggest a relatively quick tempo. If the melody of 'Banshiki Sangun', Broaching, V—IX had in early times been of the type yielded by a one-tablature-sign-to-one-*measure* reading, it is unlikely that such terms would have been applied.

Thirdly, let us consider phrasing. Up to now, we have not examined the meaning of リ in positions where it does not imply prolongation. As pointed out earlier, there is a close parallel between the metrical function of ♩ in 'Banshiki Sangun' and 'Shōenraku' and that of ⌒ in the majority of pieces in *Hakuga fue-fu* (see p. 45). Since ⌒ functions as both a phrasing-mark (defined 'interrupt the breath') and a metrical sign, it is probable, in view of other close parallels, that ♩ also has a phrasing-mark function. Indeed, inspection of the notation shows that ♩ intersects the melody line at intervals consistent with its being such a phrase-mark.

By calculating the maximum phrase-lengths marked by ♩ in sections of 'Banshiki Sangun' and 'Shōenraku', and then determining the minimum tempo at which such a phrase could be played in one breath, it is possible to determine a minimum tempo at which 'Banshiki Sangun' and 'Shōenraku' are likely to have been played.

In Prelude I—III, ♩ regularly marks off groups of six beats, and in a few instances groups of two and four beats. The minimum tempo at which a six-beat phrase could be comfortably executed on the ryūteki is about ♩ = 30. We might conclude, therefore, that these sections were played at a tempo of *at least* ♩ = 30.

In the remaining sections of Prelude IV—XII, the most common phrase-lengths are four, two, six, and eight beats. A relatively small number of phrases in excess of ten beats probably result from copyists' omissions of ♩ . If a maximum phrase-length of eight (or possibly ten) beats is accepted, a tempo in excess of *c.* ♩ = 48 (or perhaps ♩ = 66) might be appropriate for these sections.

Before considering Broaching, it should be noted that in general, in *Hakuga fue-fu*, the later movements of suites (*ha*, *sattō*, *kodatsu*) exhibit shorter phrase-lengths than earlier movements. It appears that maximum phrase-lengths in these movements do not represent the longest phrase that can be executed in one breath. Rather, shorter phrase-lengths appear to be a stylistic feature, perhaps expressing a preference for less legato phrasing consistent with the function of these later movements as dance-movements. This being so, it is difficult to determine a minimum tempo for Broaching. Nevertheless, it is likely, in view of a progressive increase in tempo in the performance of Tōgaku suites, that the later sections of 'Banshiki Sangun' were played more quickly than the Prelude, and that the tempo was in excess of ♩ = 48/66. 'Shōenraku' was probably performed at about the same tempo as 'Banshiki Sangun (Broaching)'.


In the transcription of 'Banshiki Sangun' that follows (Example 4), and in the transcription of 'Shōenraku' (Example 1, p. 44), the following conventions have been adopted:

[ ] indicates that a sign has been supplied;

( ) indicates that a sign has been ignored;

舌 notates the taiko-stroke;

V is a phrase-mark, notated in the original by the sign ♩ in positions where it does not imply prolongation.

In all the examples, the original notation is supplied below the transcription. In Example 4, important editorial emendations are indicated in footnotes following the example.

## Example 4. 'Banshiki Sangun'

**Prelude**

Section I

Section II

Section III

**Section IV**

**Section VI**

**Section VII**

**Section VIII**

**Section IX**

**Section X**

**Section XI**

**Section XII**

**Broaching**

Section I

Section II

**Section III**

**Section IV**

**Section V**

**Sections VI, VIII**

**Sections VII, IX**

**Section X**

**Notes**

(III:12 = Section III, measure 12; I,II:12 = Sections I and II, measure 12 in each; etc.)

1. See Prelude, III:2.
2. See Prelude, III:3.
3. See Prelude, III:4.
4. See Prelude, I,II:12.
5. See Prelude, I:12.
6. See Prelude, V:2.
7. Beats 5 and 6 of measure 6 in Prelude, Sections IV, V, VI should be written: 五火 亇火 六火 五 リ.
8. See Prelude, V:10.
9. These signs are omitted in the Rakusaidō copy (see p. 42) only.
10. See Prelude, IV:6.
11. The following instruction occurs at the end of Section V: 'play slowly both times'.
12. See Prelude, IV,V,IX:4.
13. See Prelude, IV,V:6.
14. See Prelude, V,VII,VIII,IX,XI:11.
15. See Prelude, VI:5.
16. See Prelude, IV,V,VII:10.
17. See Prelude, V,VI,VII:12.
18. See Prelude, IV,V,VII,VIII:10.
19. See Prelude, IV,V,VII:10.
20. See Prelude, V,VI,VII:12.
21. See Prelude, XIII:3.
22. See Prelude, IV,V,VII:10.
23. See Prelude, XII:2.
24. See Prelude, XII:3.
25. The signs 亇 乊 夕 リ are duplicated in error.
26. The sign リ occurs in this position in all sections of Broaching (but not in Prelude, Section XIII).
27. The sign リ is omitted in all sections of Broaching (but not in Prelude, Section XIII).
28. See Broaching, I,II,IV:5.
29. See Broaching, I,II,III,X:4.
30. The signs 二 リ 亇 六 are duplicated in error.
31. See Broaching, VII:2.
32. See Broaching, VII:3.
33. See Broaching, VII:8.
34. The term xucuipai/kyosaihyō (see p. 54) occurs at the end of Section V.
35. See Broaching, I,II,III,IV:7.
36. The term cuipai/saihyō (see p. 54) occurs at the end of Section VI.

37. The following instruction is written here: 'in place of Section VIII, repeat Section VI; in place of Section IX, repeat Section VII'.

38. The following term is written at the end of Section X: 'irregular beginning'.

A version of this paper was published in Japanese in *Tōyō Ongaku Kenkyū*; see Marett 1978b.

## Bibliography

Condit, J. 1976. 'Differing transcriptions from the twelfth century Japanese koto manuscript *Jinchi Yōroku*', *Ethnomusicology* XX no. 1

Garfias, R. 1975. *Music of a Thousand Autumns*, Berkeley, Calif.

Gimm, M. 1966. *Das Yueh-fu tsa-lu des Tuan An Chieh*, Wiesbaden

*Hakuga fue-fu*: (a) copy in the Rakusaidō collection of the Research Archives for Japanese Music, Ueno Gakuen University, Tokyo; (b) copy in the Tokyo University of the Arts, catalogue number 1363 16.15.1.1

Harich-Schneider, E. 1973. *A history of Japanese music*, Oxford

*Kogakusho ishu*, published by Tenri Toshokan, 1971

Marett, A. 1976. 'Hakuga's flute score', unpublished Ph.D. dissertation, Cambridge

Marett, A. 1977. 'Tunes notated in flute tablature from a Japanese source of the tenth century', *Musica Asiatica* I, Oxford

Marett, A. 1978a. 'Hakuga fue-fu no sho-kifuhō ni tsuite' (Differing notations in *Hakuga fue-fu*), *Gagaku-kai* no. 54, Tokyo

Marett, A. 1978b. 'Hakuga fue-fu no Tōgaku-kyoku Banshiki Sangun ni tsuite' ('Banshiki Sangun': a piece from the Tōgaku repertory of Japanese court music preserved in *Hakuga fue-fu*), *Tōyō Ongaku Kenkyū* no. 43

Picken, L.E.R. 1956. Report to *Ethnomusicology Newsletter* 6

Picken, L.E.R. 1966. 'Secular Chinese songs of the twelfth century', in *Studia Musicologica Academicae Scientiorum Hungaricae* VIII

Picken, L.E.R. 1967. 'Central Asian tunes in the gagaku tradition', in *Festschrift Walter Wiora*, Kassel

Picken, L.E.R. 1969. 'Tunes apt for T'ang lyrics from the Shō partbooks of Togaku', in *Essays in ethnomusicology: a birthday offering for Lee Hye-ku*, Seoul

Shiba, S. 1972. *Gosen-fu ni yoru gagaku sōfu*, Tokyo

## Glossary

ampu-hō 案 譜 法
aitake 合 竹
banshiki 盤 涉
Banshiki Sangun 盤 涉 参 軍
biwa 琵 琶
Bonryūshū no jo 汎 龍 舟 序
Chū Ōga ryūteki yōroku-fu 註 大 神 龍 笛 要 錄 譜
cui 催
cuipai 催 拍
daqu 大 曲
gagaku 雅 楽
Gakufu Zatsuroku 楽 府 雜 錄
gaku-sō 楽 箏
ha 破
Hakuchū 白 柱
Hakuga fue-fu 博 雅 笛 譜
hayagaki 早 搔
Heian 平 安
hichiriki 篳 篥
hyōshi 拍 子
Jinchi yōroku 仁 知 要 錄
jissai 實 催
jissaihyō 實 催 拍
jo 序
jō 帖
jū 重
Kaichū-fu 懷 中 譜
kobyōshi 小 拍 子
kodatsu 褌 脱
Kosō-fu 古 箏 譜
kyosai 虛 催
kyosaihyō 虛 催 拍
Minamoto no Hiromasa 源 博 雅
Moto uta 元 歌
Ōshiki 黄 鍾
paizi 拍 子
po 破
Rakusaidō 楽 歲 堂
ryūteki 龍 笛

sai 催
Saibara 催馬楽
saihyō 催拍
sattō 颯踏
shicui 實催
shicuipai 實催拍
shizugaki 閑搔
shō 笙
Shōenraku 承燕楽
taiko 大鼓
taikyoku 大曲
Taizoku-kaku-banshiki-chō Choka-Manzairaku 大蔟角盤渉譜鳥萬歳楽
Tang 唐
Tenri 天理
Tōgaku 唐楽
Tokubanji 德伴字
Toyohara no Tomoaki 豊原倫秋
Ueno Gakuen 上野学園
xucui 虚催
xucuipai 虚催拍
Yuefu zalu 楽府雜錄

# Tang-music (Tōgaku) manuscripts for lute and their interrelationships

REMBRANDT WOLPERT

In another publication (Wolpert: in press (a)), I have demonstrated the virtual identity in melodic outline between a version of the piece 'Chongming yue / Sōmeiraku' in a Japanese source of Tang date (the *Wuxian pu / Gogen-fu*,[1] hereafter cited as *WXP*) for five-stringed lute, and a version for four-stringed lute in the twelfth-century Japanese lute score *Sango-yōroku*[2] (hereafter *SGYR*). The two versions differ only in that the version in *SGYR* is conspicuously ornamented.

Further pieces preserved in *WXP* are also represented in *SGYR*, for instance 'Wang Zhao jun / Ōshōkun',[3] 'Yeban yue / Yahanraku', and 'Yinjiu yue / Onjuraku'. Between the versions of these in *WXP* and *SGYR* there are substantial differences in structure but not in basic melodic materials. In general, the *WXP* versions are longer than those in *SGYR*. 'Yeban yue' and 'Yinjiu yue' are modally the same in *WXP* and *SGYR* versions, but the version of 'Wang Zhao jun' in *WXP* is Mixolydian, while that in *SGYR* is Dorian. However, in each case the two versions (*WXP* and *SGYR*) are undoubtedly the same piece. Compare, for instance, the opening phrase in the piece 'Wang Zhao jun' in *WXP* with the corresponding opening phrase in *SGYR*, as shown in Example 1.

A detailed comparison of the related pieces in *WXP* and *SGYR* will be made on a later occasion. A preliminary examination has revealed that the sample of Tang-music pieces

Example 1

1  For bibliographical details see Hayashi 1969: 138–201; Harich-Schneider 1973: 85f; Wolpert, in press (a).
2  For bibliographical details see Harich-Schneider 1973: 273; Wolpert 1977: 113; and Markham, in preparation.
3  For the historical background of this piece see Wolpert 1977: 134.

present in both *WXP* and *SGYR* is small. However, the relationship between items common to the two sources justifies the conclusion that while versions in *SGYR* may differ in formal structure and in mode from versions of Tang date, they are nevertheless closely related to Tang originals, and in melodic style and material they are identical.

A comparison of versions for four-stringed lute of Tang-music pieces in *SGYR* with versions for the same instrument in later manuscripts shows that the differences between these later versions and *SGYR* are minimal.

As already shown (Wolpert 1977: 113), the functions of primary and secondary tablature signs (the former indicating string and fret positions, the latter mensural organisation) in lute manuscripts have scarcely changed since the earliest surviving lute manuscripts, the *Tempyō biwa-fu* (see Hayashi 1969: 124–34 and Wolpert 1975: 34ff), *WXP*, and the *Fushiminomiya-bon biwa-fu* (see Wolpert 1977). Such changes as are to be observed are by way of the addition of elements of mensural notation, superimposed on the mensural system of the earliest manuscripts. The additional elements may conveniently be referred to as tertiary tablature signs (Wolpert 1975: 34ff, 47ff and 197ff).

In the oldest manuscripts (of Tang date), the secondary tablature signs *huo* 火 (halving the note value), *yin* 引 (doubling the note value), and *ting* 丁 (rest), and the notation of orna-mental notes as small tablature signs, to be executed within the same beat as the main note (Wolpert 1977: 112ff and 121f), permit an unambiguous reading of the tablature. These early manuscripts are sparsely ornamented.

In *SGYR*, however, we are suddenly confronted with extensive notated ornamentation (Wolpert, in press (b)). To facilitate the reading of a now more complex tablature in which columns of notes are often extended by the interpolation of glosses, new mensural notation provided by the tertiary tablature signs has been added. This consists of three additional metrical systems, superimposed both on each other and on the old system. These systems are:

(1) The indication of the main drum-beat of the large drum dagu/taiko within the measure by writing the sign *bai* 百 [4] to the right of the appropriate tablature sign. In Tang-music the main drum-beat falls regularly on the third beat in a measure of four beats (4/4), and on the fifth beat (occasionally on the seventh beat) in a measure of eight beats (8/8).[5]

(2) The marking-off of two-beat segments of notation by intracolumnary dots or circles. The intracolumnary dots/circles, together with the indications given by the secondary tablature signs from the old system of metrical notation, unambiguously define the mensural structure of the music and facilitate the reading of the tablature. This system of intracolumnary dots/circles is of purely mensural function.

(3) The indication of the beats of the hour-glass drum jiegu/kakko by small extracolumnary dots written to the right of the tablature signs. In Tang-music these dots also indicate segments of one beat in duration.[5] This value is clear from the three other systems, including the – in some sense 'primary' – mensural system of secondary tablature signs.

4   A graphic abbreviation of the character *pai* 拍 'beat'; see Picken 1974: 12.
5   This does not apply to the Saibara and Komagaku repertories, also included in *SGYR*; cf. Markham, in preparation.

In the absence of extracolumnary dots, the metrical structure of the piece is made explicit by the intracolumnary dots/circles of the binary system. These intracolumnary dots/circles are retained even in versions with extracolumnary dots; the latter mark half-units in the intra-columnary dot/circle system,[6] but do not add to rhythmic certainty or modify the reading of the tablature in any way. Their primary function is evidently that of a notation for percussion.[7]

The manuscripts listed here — used to show the unbroken tradition of Tang-music manu-scripts from the twelfth century to the present day — all employ the same system of primary, secondary, and tertiary tablature signs. The particular manuscripts have been selected both be-cause the originals, or photographic copies, are all available in the Picken Collection in the Uni-versity Library, Cambridge, and because they are all dated[8] and provide us with sources three centuries apart from each other in date of compilation.

The three manuscripts are:

(1) *SGYR*

(2) A scroll dated 1566 and simply entitled *Biwa-fu*[9] (hereafter *BF*) which, because of its convenient length, has been transcribed in full and has provided me with the selection of pieces for comparison.[10]

(3) The *Meiji biwa-fu* (hereafter *Meiji*), dated 1876 and compiled by the musicians of the Japanese Imperial Court. This source is still in use today.[11]

Where there are several different versions for the same piece in the same manuscript, all the versions have been transcribed and compared to show their interrelationship.[12] The result of this latter comparison will be discussed elsewhere (Wolpert, in press (b)).

To demonstrate the identical use of tertiary tablature signs in the three manuscripts (*SGYR*, *BF*, and *Meiji*), the piece 'Yuedian yue / Etenraku' (the final item in the transcriptions, pp.

---

6   This again applies only to Tang-music; for the sole function of this system of extracolumn-ary dots as a notation for percussion in Saibara see Markham, in preparation. In Komagaku, extracolumnary dots occur at two-beat intervals and the system of intracolumnary dots is not used.

7   See *Taigenshō* 602; also Markham, in preparation.

8   There exists an abundance of undated Tang-music manuscripts, dateable either by compar-ing style of script, type of paper etc. or by using internal evidence such as names of historical persons mentioned in preface or colophon. As an example of the scope of one of these un-dated manuscripts and their contents, a lute-score, the *Biwa Saibara-fu* (preserved in the Picken Collection, University Library, Cambridge), probably of early Edo (A.D. 1603—1868) date, has been transcribed in full in Wolpert 1975: 238—301.

9   For bibliographical details see Picken and Wolpert, in press.

10  This was the first manuscript shown to me by Dr Picken when I became his pupil in 1972. Inclusion in this article of a complete transcription of *BF* — the oldest of the original manuscripts in the Picken Collection — seems appropriate.

11  A complete transcription of *Meiji* can be found in Wolpert 1975: 302—63.

12  *Tempyō biwa-fu* and *Fushiminomiya-bon biwa-fu* have been set out in comparative tran-scription with *SGYR* in Wolpert 1977: 151—6.

Example 2. 'Yuedian yue / Etenraku'

73–119) is set out in Example 2 with the sign 百 , intracolumnary dots/circles, and small extracolumnary dots to the right included as they occur.

Tertiary tablature signs are not included in the transcriptions, but for all items their use in the manuscripts is precisely as shown in Example 2.

From these two demonstrations — namely, a comparison of a manuscript of Tang date (*WXP*) with a manuscript from the late twelfth century (*SGYR*), and a comparison of the same twelfth-century manuscript with two manuscripts from the sixteenth and late nineteenth centuries respectively — the following conclusions may be drawn:

(1) that between the ninth and twelfth centuries, tunes notated in lute tablatures remained essentially the same;

(2) that during the same period, extensive notated ornamentation was added;

(3) that in *SGYR*, to facilitate the reading of a now more complex tablature, new systems of mensural notation have been superimposed upon the earlier system; and

(4) that the system of notation exhibited by *SGYR* has remained unchanged to the present day.

The Tang-music manuscripts for lute thus present an unbroken tradition of sources extending over more than 1100 years.

Example 3

皇麞・破

SGYR

BF

八帖

end of 八帖 in *BF* (1566)

九帖

急

半
帖

79

五常楽

序

破

SGYR

BF

Meiji

* One beat (g) omitted because of metric structure (8 beats–bar)
† The repeat has been written out in this ms; the last beat in the repeat is B♯.

夫南

武昌楽　道行 朝小子
三太平楽道行

太平楽

破

SGYR

1

2

Meiji

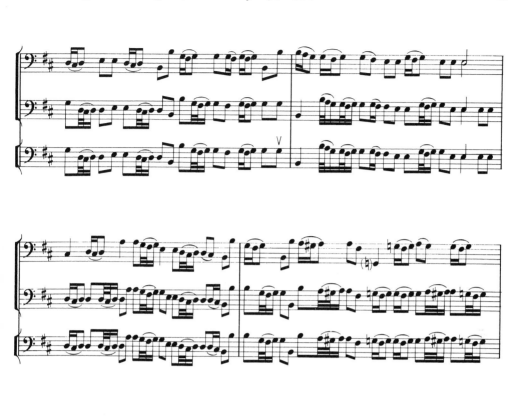

太平楽

急

甘 州

\* alternative versions to *SGYR* 1.

想 夫 戀

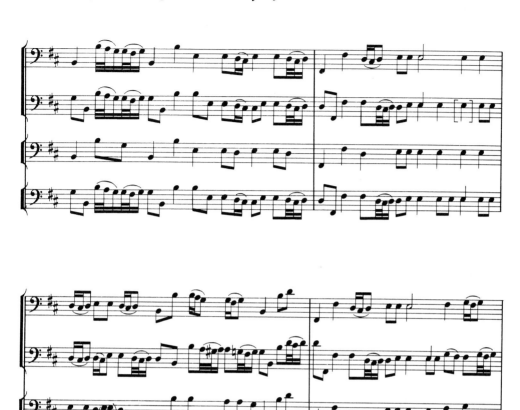

An additional clef-sign has been added to facilitate comparison. Versions in the bass clef are always the straight transcriptions from manuscripts; C-clefs are used for purposes of transposition for comparison only.

‾‾‾ indicates intercolumnary dots     ‾‾‾ indicates phrase mark     * indicates end of the intercolumnary dots

* marks end of dots to the right and return to the intercolumnary dots.

蘇合香　三帖

SGYR

BF

Meiji

[Repeat marked as such–not written out in extenso.]

[see SGYR 1]

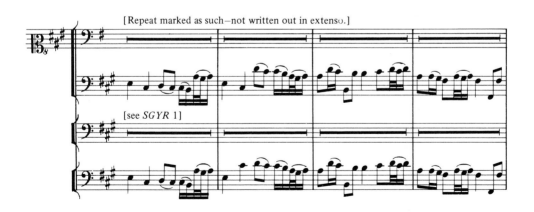

* one superfluous dot omitted.

† one missing dot supplied: parallel version confirms placing of missing dot. As a result of the repeating of the same error in *SGYR* 2 and later mss the main beat is moving forward in the bar at each repeat. *SGYR* 1 preserves the version free of this error.

99

* 'new creation' of the tablature sign ⼦ —but most likely a writing mistake.

蘇合香　四帖

* marks end of intercolumnary dots and beginning of dots to the right.
† from here onwards same as in 'sanjo'. 三帖. 以下同五帖

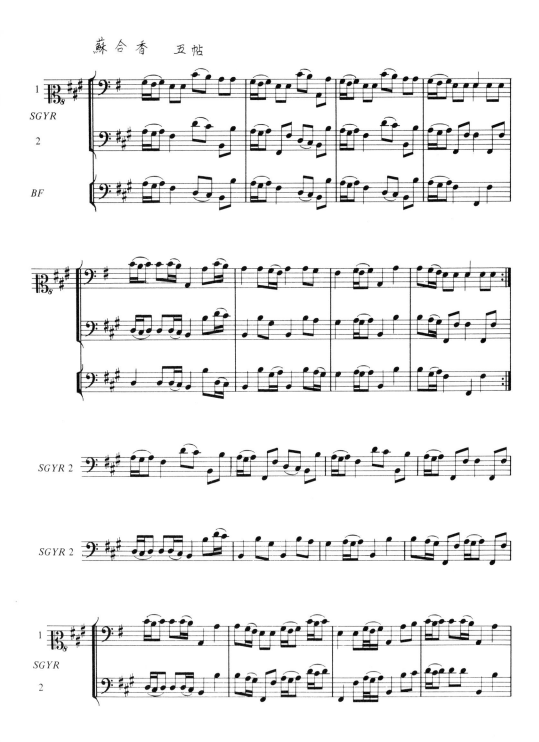

蘇合香　五帖

蘇合香 破

Fine

dal segno 同 al Fine.

109

蘇合香　急

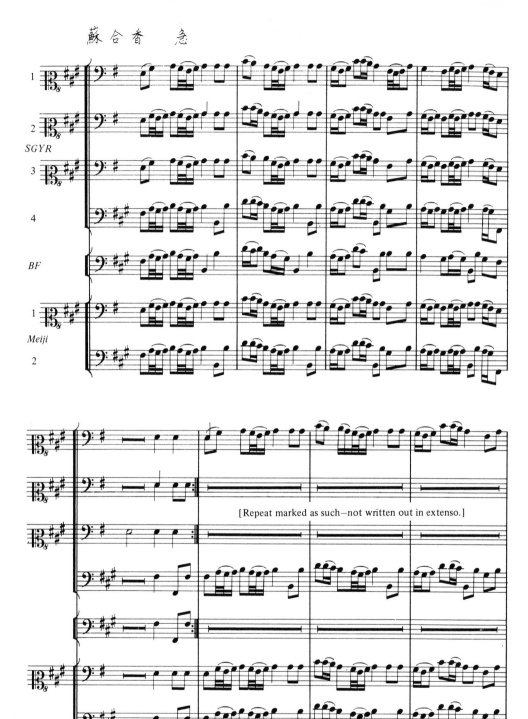

[Repeat marked as such—not written out in extenso.]

嗩頭

2nd time
ends
here.

白柱

The piece is notated in two different tunings in *SGYR*. To facilitate comparison an additional key signature has been added.

Tuning *SGYR* 1: ; *SGYR* 2, *BF* and *Meiji*:

青 海 波

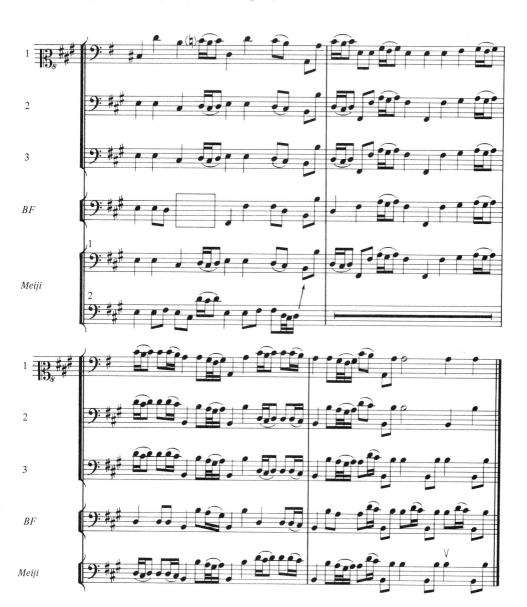

千秋楽

越殿楽

* Probably a copyist's mistake ヒ = G♮ instead of 七 = F♯.

## Bibliography

### Books and articles

Harich-Schneider, E. 1973. *A history of Japanese music*, London

Hayashi, Kenzō 1969. 'Tempyō biwa-fu "Bankasō" no kaisetsu' 天 平 琵 琶 譜「番 伎 崇 」の 解 譜 and 'Kokuhō gogen-fu to sono kaidoku no tancho' 国 宝 五 絃 譜 と そ の 解 読 の 端 緒 , *Gagaku* 雅 楽 , Tokyo, pp. 124—34 and 138—201

Markham, E.J., in preparation. 'Saibara —Japanese court songs of the Heian period', *Würzburger Sino-Japonica*, Wiesbaden

Picken, L.E.R. 1972. 'Tenri toshokan shozō na jūyō no Tōgaku-fu ni kansuru oboeki' 天 理 書 館 所 蔵 の 重 要 な 唐 楽 譜 に 関 す る 覚 書, *Biblia* 57, Tokyo

Picken, L.E.R. and Wolpert, R.F., in press. 'Mouth-organ and lute parts of Tōgaku and their interrelationships', *Musica Asiatica* III, Oxford

Taigenshō 體 源 鈔 , ed. Nihon koten zenshū, Tokyo 1933

Wolpert, R.F. 1975. 'Lute music and tablatures of the Tang period', unpublished Ph.D. dissertation, Cambridge

Wolpert, R.F. 1977. 'A ninth-century Sino-Japanese lute tutor', *Musica Asiatica* I, Oxford

Wolpert, R.F., in press (a). 'A ninth-century score for five-stringed lute', *Musica Asiatica* III, Oxford

Wolpert, R.F., in press (b). 'The evolution of notated ornamentation in Tang-music manuscripts', in *Festschrift Herbert Franke* (ed. W. Bauer), Munich

### Lute manuscripts

*Biwa-fu* 琵 琶 譜 . Manuscript in Kikutei-bon Gagaku-sho 菊 亭 本 雅 楽 書 Collection, now part of the Picken Collection, University Library, Cambridge

*Biwa-fu, Biwa Saibara fu* 琵 琶 譜 , 琵 琶 催 馬 楽 譜 Manuscript in Kikutei-bon Gagaku-sho 菊 亭 本 雅 楽 書 Collection, now part of the Picken Collection, University Library, Cambridge

*Fushiminomiya-bon-biwa-fu* 伏 見 宮 本 琵 琶 譜 . Manuscript in Kunaichō Shoryōbu 宮 内 庁 書 陵 部 . Facsimile in University Library, Cambridge, catalogued as FH 99032

*Gogen-fu* 五 絃 譜 . Manuscript in Yōmei Bunko 陽 明 文 學 . Microfilm in Picken Collection, University Library, Cambridge

*Meiji biwa-fu* 明 治 琵 琶 譜 . Manuscript of Imperial Household. Photocopy in Picken Collection, University Library, Cambridge

*Sango-yōroku* 三 五 要 録 . Compiled by Fujiwara Moronaga 藤 原 師 長. Original manuscript is to be dated between 1171 and 1192. Copy of 1328 in Kunaichō Shoryōbu 宮 内 庁 書 陵 部 . Microfilm in Picken Collection, University Library, Cambridge

*Tempyō-biwa-fu* 天 平 琵 琶 譜 . A photographic reproduction of this fragment is to be found in Kishibe, Shigeo *et al.*, *Shōsōin no gakki* 正 倉 院 の 楽 器 , Tokyo 1967, pl. 119

**Glossary**

'Chongming yue / Sōmeiraku' 崇明楽
dagu/taiko 大鼓
jiegu/kakko 羯鼓
'Wang Zhaoju / Ōshōkun' 王昭君
'Yeban yue / Yahanraku' 夜半楽
'Yinjiu yue / Onjuraku' 飲酒楽
'Yuedian yue / Etenraku' 越殿楽

# Some melodic features of Chinese qin music

YOKO MITANI

I. Metrical structure and phrasing
II. Rhythmic features
III. Changes in the tuning system
IV. The relationship between tunings and melodies

The Chinese qin, a seven-stringed zither, is the oldest and most important long-zither in the Far East. Its music has maintained a unique position in the history of Chinese music. The origin of the qin and qin music can be traced back to remote antiquity. During the Han dynasty (206 B.C.–A.D. 220) and after, it was highly developed as a member of the orchestra for Confucian ceremonies and court music, and as a solo instrument played by noblemen and literati.

The main features of the instrument are the elegant shape of its black-lacquered body (see Figure 1) and the delicate and subtle nuances of its sounds. It is assumed that the number of strings was originally five, which represented the five tones of the Chinese pentatonic scale. Later, probably in the Zhou period (1122–255 B.C.), two more strings were added. The basic tuning of the seven strings is pentatonic, and the two highest strings (the sixth and the seventh) are tuned, as a rule, one octave higher than the two lowest strings (the first and the second).

From ancient times qin solo music was developed as a sort of programme music, in which each melodic pattern or even a single note has its own significance and is intended to evoke a special reaction in the listener's mind. After a long tradition through the Tang (A.D. 618–906) and Song (960–1278) dynasties, qin music flourished in the early years of the Ming (1368–1644) dynasty, by which time the finger techniques, the tunings, and the notational system were perfected. Also, the special ideology of qin music, qindao, had been established on the basis of Confucianism, Taoism, and Buddhism.

Innumerable masterpieces of qin music are preserved in the 'notation of abbreviated characters', *jianzi pu*, in the qin handbooks compiled in the Ming and Qing (1644–1911) periods (see Figure 2). Unfortunately, however, only a few pieces dating from before the Ming dynasty are extant in written form. One of them is 'Jieshi diao yulan', which was written in a sentence-notational system in the Tang period and has been preserved in Kyoto, Japan. Others are Jiang

Figure 1. Playing the qin (from *Qinxue rumen*, 1864)

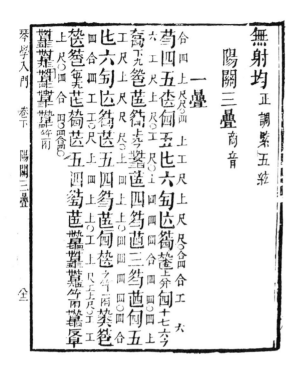

Figure 2. Jianzi pu from *Qinxue rumen*

Kui's 'Guyuan' (*c.* 1202) (see Picken 1971) and some short pieces contained in *Shilin guangji* (1269), all of which are notated in jianzi pu.

Nearly three hundred qin pieces composed in the Ming dynasty have been handed down to the present day, many of which are of high artistic value; and more than thirty qin handbooks were compiled during this period. It is in this period that qin music was developed as a result of an artistic impulse to praise the beauty and power of nature. The composers could freely create very original and attractive tunes using a variety of tunings and sophisticated finger techniques.

Although more than sixty-five qin handbooks were published during the 267 years of the Qing dynasty, the creative activity of qin music did not flourish as it had done in the previous dynasty. But it is a distinguishing feature of this period that theoretical and critical research into qin music and the compilation of enormous works of literary materials were firmly established. The tunings and the tunes of the Ming dynasty and before were re-examined and re-arranged systematically by means of five authentic pentatonic modes (see pp. 134f.).

The number of qin pieces which are actually performed today is limited. But the delicate beauty of qin music is still immutably attractive to listeners. In the following pages some melodic features of qin music are considered in relation to its metrical structure, rhythm, and tunings.

## I. Metrical structure and phrasing

One outstanding feature of qin music is that the metre and rhythm are rarely notated in jianzi pu manuscripts, but depend almost entirely on the performer's interpretation. Therefore, the same original qin melody can give rise to different versions. Example 1 is a comparative transcription of six versions of the first section of a famous qin piece, 'Yangguan sandie' ('The parting at Yangguan').[1] The composer is anonymous, but the text is based on a well-known poem of Wang Wei (699–759), a famous poet of the Tang period. The musical setting for qin, in which the poem may originally have been sung by the player (cf. Lieberman 1975), is assumed to date from the end of the Song dynasty. The qin melody has been printed in twenty-seven different qin handbooks since the end of the fifteenth century.

The six versions in Example 1 probably derive from the same tradition, that of *Qinxue rumen* (1864), one of the most representative qin handbooks. The fundamental melodic lines (except ornaments) are coincident, but the metrical structure and rhythm are considerably different from each other. Table 1 shows that text-phrases 2–5 all have seven syllables each, but are set to different numbers of musical beats, in the same and in different versions.

Table 1

| | phrase 2 | phrase 3 | phrase 4 | phrase 5 |
|---|---|---|---|---|
| no. of syllables | 7 | 7 | 7 | 7 |
| no. of beats: version 1: | 6 | 7 | 6 | 6 |
| version 2: | 4 | 8 | 4 | 6 |
| version 3: | 5 | 9 | 5 | 6 |
| version 4: | 6 | $7\frac{1}{2}$ | $5\frac{1}{2}$ | 6 |
| version 5: | 5 | $6\frac{1}{2}$ | $4\frac{1}{2}$ | $4\frac{1}{2}$ |
| version 6: | 6 | 8 | 8 | 6 |

In the six versions of the melody, the number of beats in the second, third and fourth phrases varies; the fifth phrase is played in six beats by five performers of the six. (A half-beat occurs frequently in versions 4 and 5; it is likely that the performer unconsciously lengthens or shortens a beat.) Apart from this irregularity in the number of beats, some common features can be seen among the six versions: (a) each phrase of the text is coincident with a melodic

1   (1) The tradition of Xia Yifeng, from Yang Yinliu and Hou Zuowu 1956, vol. I.
    (2) As performed by Guan Pinghu, transcribed *Guqin quji*, vol. I.
    (3) Transcribed by Yang Yinliu 1956, vol. I.
    (4) Performed by Wang Zhenhua in 1967, transcribed in *Guqin quji*, vol. I.
    (5) Performed by Wei Zhonglao, Lyrichord LL72, transcribed by the author.
    (6) Played and sung by Pan Qi, Columbia S6002-A, transcribed by the author.

Example 1. 'Yangguan sandie', first section

清 和 節 當 春. 渭 城 朝 雨 浥 輕 塵. 客 舍 青 青

柳 色 新 勸君更盡 一 盃 酒. 西 出 陽 關 無 故 人.

*Note:* ⟋ and ⌢ indicate articulation by movement of the left hand (see note 2).

phrase; (b) the time-value of the last note of each phrase is prolonged, usually to two beats; and (c) the last note of each phrase is, in many cases, one of the significant notes of the mode: tonic, dominant, or subdominant. Feature (a) is also found in other qin pieces which seem to have been originally composed as vocal pieces and still preserve a text even after they have ceased to be sung.

Features (b) and (c) can also be seen in purely instrumental qin pieces. There, however, the length of a melodic phrase is more irregular because it is not restricted by that of a phrase of the text. Very frequently melodic phrases in instrumental pieces are expanded by means of rhythmic or melodic patterns produced by sophisticated finger techniques.[2] As seen in

Example 2. 'Gaoshan liushui', tenth section

2  Qin finger techniques are discussed in English by van Gulik 1939: 120–33; Lui Tsun-yuen 1966: 185–200; Kaufmann 1967: 279–92; in Chinese by Wang Guangqi 1931: 23–49; Shen Zaonong *et al.* 1961: 26–44; and in Japanese by Mitani 1974: 22–8. [In playing the qin the strings are plucked with the right hand and stopped with the left against the body of the instrument: see Figure 1. Notes can also be made to sound, but more delicately, by striking or sliding with the left-hand fingers and thumb. – Editor]

Example 2, the tenth section of 'Gaoshan liushui',[3] such techniques as *kun* and *fu* (glissando) or *dayuan* (repetition of the same pitch played by plucking with the right-hand index and middle fingers alternately) are an essential part of the metrical or melodic structure of instrumental pieces.

When qin pieces are transcribed into Western notation, a time signature of 2/4, 3/4, or 4/4 is used for convenience. But qin music is not based on the Western stressed accent, and therefore it cannot be automatically divided into measures using bar-lines. We may conclude that the metrical structure of qin music consists of phrases of unequal length in binary time, ternary time, or a combination of both.

## II. Rhythmic features

The metre and rhythm of qin music can be decided by the performer as he likes, but fundamentally he interprets one *jianzi* (one tablature sign) as one beat (transcribed as a crotchet). One beat is further divided into smaller time units as follows:

Notes of smaller time value are usually produced by finger techniques of the left hand and in many cases appear as passing notes.

On the other hand one beat is frequently combined with another beat, making a two-beat tonal pattern.

These one-beat and two-beat tonal patterns are a fundamental rhythmic element in qin music, but many patterns of more than two beats, produced by special finger techniques, are effectively used. These patterns, shown in Example 3, are produced by using the fingers of both right and left hands, the tones yielded by the left hand being weaker in volume and more subtle in timbre than those of the right hand. This delicate contrast affects the melodic and rhythmic structure of qin music.

Both the metre and the rhythm of qin music differ according to qin schools or individual performers. Example 4 is a comparative score of two versions of 'Oulu wangji' as performed by

3  Performed and transcribed by Hou Zuowu, following the tradition of *Tianwenge qin pu jicheng* (1876); Yang Yinliu and Hou Zuowu 1956, vol. 1.

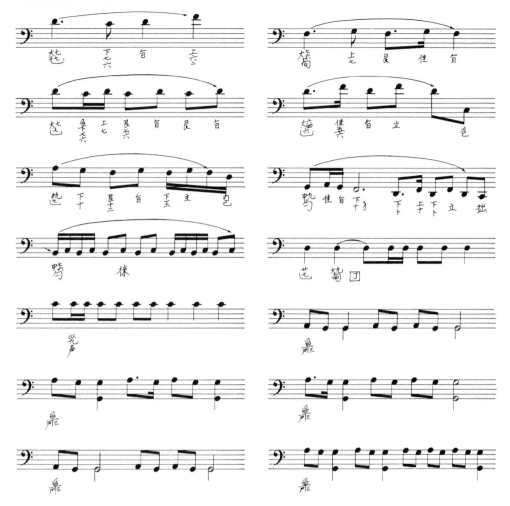

Example 3. The patterns produced by special finger techniques

two different players, based on the same piece notated in the qin handbook *Ziyuantang qin pu* (1802). (1) is a version played by Zha Fuxi and (2) by Guan Pinghu.[4]

The differences in metre and rhythm are as follows:

(a) The metrical structure is basically binary in (1) and (2).

(b) In (1), bars 9, 12, 13, 14, and 20 have three beats and bars 10 and 19 have four. In (2), bars 16 and 19 have three beats and bars 11 and 13 have five. These bars of more than two beats mainly consist of the tonal patterns produced by special finger techniques.

(c) The performer of (1) prefers dotted rhythms such as ♩. ♪ or ♩. ♫ , and the performer of (2) smoother rhythms such as ♩ ♩ , or ♫ .

(d) In (2), right-hand glissando (as in bar 1) is played faster than in (1).

4  Transcribed in *Guqin quji*.

131

Example 4. 'Oulu wangji', first section

These rhythmic variations arise from the differences of rhythmic interpretation or taste in the individual performer and reflect his personality. Needless to say, however, such individual interpretation of rhythm must always display the original content of a qin piece. The importance of this can be seen by looking at 'Guangling san'.

'Guangling san', the compilation of which is attributed to Xi Kang (223–62), is one of the masterpieces in the history of qin music. The subject matter, handed down from the Han dynasty, is the hero's vengeance on the king for his father's death. It is necessary, therefore, that the performer should interpret its rhythm properly to represent the contents: the hero's sorrow, anger, or psychological tension. In Example 5, (1) and (2) are taken from the nineteenth section, 'Changhong' ('A long rainbow'), and (3) and (4) from the twenty-first section, 'Fanu' ('Rage'). (1) and (3) are transcribed according to the performance of Guan Pinghu, and (2) and (4) that of Zhang Shibin.[5] Mr. Guan prefers a rather smooth rhythmic structure: ♩. ♩ ♩ ♩ ♩ ♩ in (1)A, ♪ ♪♪♩ ♩ ♩ in (3)B, and ♪ ♩ ♪♩ ♩ ♩ ♪ in (3)C, whereas Mr Zhang tries to

Example 5. 'Guangling san', from *Shenji bipu* (1425)

5  (1) and (3) transcribed in *Guangling san*; (2) and (4) transcribed from the notation of
   Zhang Shibin by the author.

represent the contents in a stiff rhythmic structure: ♪ ♩ ♪ ♪ ♩. in (2)A, ♪ ♩ ♪ ♪ ♩ ♩ in (4)B, and ♫ ♩. ♬ ♫ ♪ in (4)C. Considering the subject matter of this piece, Mr Zhang's interpretation of the rhythm seems to be more suitable.

Thus, rhythmic structure plays a very important rôle in qin music, because the rhythm can clearly display the atmosphere of the composition and the feelings or emotions of the composer or the performer.

### III. Changes in the tuning system

After the Song dynasty the number of tunings of the qin greatly increased. In the Song period there were two types of tuning, according to the introductory note to 'Guyuan' (see above p. 125). One is a type called *zhenglong*, being five authentic tunings that consist of a pentatonic scale and therefore do not contain any chromatic notes (see Example 6). The other is a type called *cilong*, three plagal or irregular modes which contain one or two chromatic notes in the tuning. The tuning of 'Guyuan' is called cishang diao, belonging to the cilong type. It is tuned by lowering by a semitone, the third, fourth, and sixth strings of zheng diao tuning: C D F G A c d (zheng diao) is changed into C D E F♯ A B d (cishang diao). In the latter the sixth string does not make an octave with the first. Zhenglong corresponds to the five regular modes, and cilong to the *wai diao*, irregular modes derived from zhengdiao, of the Ming dynasty.

The number of wai diao increased by the beginning of the Ming period (1368–1644). About thirty wai diao tunings are mentioned in the qin handbooks, published from the beginning of the fifteenth century until the latter half of the eighteenth century, such as *Taigu yiyin*, *Qin pu zhengzhuan*, and *Ziyuantang qin pu*. It seems that in those days all the tunings, except for zheng diao, were called wai diao. Therefore, four other regular tunings, consisting of a pentatonic scale, were included among the wai diao. Although theoretically there existed many wai diao tunings, the number of tunings actually used was limited; five regular tunings and some not-so-irregular wai diao were popular.

Names, according to *Qinxue rumen* (1864)

zhonglü jun (Song: zheng diao)

wushi jun

jiazhong jun

yici jun

huangzhong jun

Example 6. Five authentic tunings

In the Ming handbooks each group of pieces belonging to the same mode was preceded by its own *diaoyi*: a short musical composition which indicates a fixed melodic pattern, characteristic of the mode, and fixed finger techniques (see Liang 1975). Therefore, a diaoyi is played in order to prepare both player and listener for the main composition which follows and to create the proper atmosphere for each mode. Although the tunes in the Ming dynasty handbooks differ greatly, each tune belonging to the same mode usually finishes with a short ending melody derived from the appropriate diaoyi. Therefore, it is possible to say that the diaoyi form a common factor, and that they have a close functional relationship with the main compositions.

In the middle of the Qing dynasty (1644–1911) a change occurred in the tunings of the qin. The wai diao were adjusted and unified into five authentic modes, with some exceptions: for instance, manshang diao, C C F G A c d, for 'Guangling san', cishang diao (see p. 134) for 'Guyuan'. According to the adjustment of the tunings, the compositions themselves were rearranged, and some very peculiar and unpopular tunes given in the Ming handbooks were forgotten in the latter half of the Qing dynasty. Another characteristic feature of the pieces notated in the Qing dynasty handbooks is that in many cases a short cadence, *weisheng*, is played at the end of a piece in harmonics (*fanyin*), instead of the ending melody displaying characteristics of the diaoyi commonly found in the pieces of the Ming handbooks (see above).

This adjustment and unification of the qin tunings may reflect a general tendency of scientific and theoretical study in the latter half of the Qing dynasty.

We should not overlook, however, the confusion over the present terminology concerning the five authentic tunings. *Qinxue rumen* (1864) and its school gave them the names of zhonglü jun, wushi jun, jiazhong jun, yici jun, and huangzhong jun (see Example 6). A more modern handbook, *Meian qin pu* (1931), and its school, call them respectively huangzhong diao, zhonglü diao, wushi diao, taicu diao and linzhong diao. Some modern performers prefer to use the names of the old waidiao for the five authentic tunings.[6] Thus, the present terminology differs according to the handbooks and the genealogy of the tradition.


## IV. The relationship between tunings and melodies

In the Ming dynasty, as mentioned above, in addition to the five authentic tunings, a number of irregular wai diao were used. Because of this variety of tunings, qin melodies which seem to have derived from the same original were notated in various handbooks in different tunings. For instance, the tunings of 'Yangguan sandie' (or 'Yangguan qu'), which is preserved in twenty-seven qin handbooks, are jiliang diao, ruibin diao, and wushi jun. The early versions of 'Yang-guan sandie' are written in jilang diao and modern versions in wushi jun, which is identical to ruibin diao. The jiliang diao tuning, one of the irregular modes (wai diao), consists of C Eb F G Bb c d, and wushi jun of C D F G Bb c d. They are different from each other only in the pitch of the second string: the second and seventh strings of the jiliang diao tuning do not make an octave. The versions of 'Yangguan sandie' appearing in the Ming and early Qing handbooks are mainly composed in jiliang diao, but very rarely contain the open string Eb of this tuning. Example 7 shows the first section of various versions of this piece.[7] Since it is not easy (and not necessary in this case) to transcribe the tunes with rhythm, they are shown only in pitch.

In this example, the tunings of (1), (2), (4), and (5) are jiliang diao, and that of (3) is ruibin diao. The characteristic note of the second string of the former tuning, Eb, appears only in bar 2 of (1), bar 1 of (2), and bar 3 of (4), all of which are produced by the open second string. Thus, though very rarely, Eb of the second string can be seen in the Ming manuscripts. However, in version (5), from Tōkō-kin-pu (1865, originally compiled by Sigiura Kinzen in the early eighteenth century) the note Eb does not appear, though its tuning is jiliang diao. Comparing this version with that of Qinxue rumen (cf. Example 1), which became standard from the late Qing period and whose tuning is wushi jun, we find that both versions are somewhat similar and do not contain any note produced on the open second string. The second string is used by being stopped at the eleventh stud in Tōkō-kin-pu, and at the tenth stud in Qinxue rumen, both of which produce the same note, G. Table 2 shows how this note is differently notated in the two sources. Thus, by changing the stud at which a note is to be stopped, the same tune can be played in different tunings.


6   Cf. Shen Zaonong *et al.* 1961.
7   (1) 'Yangguan sandie', *Zheyin shizi qin pu* (before 1491), and 'Yangguan', *Faming qin pu* (1530).
    (2) 'Yangguan sandie', *Faming qin pu.*
    (3) 'Yangguan', *Fengxuan xuanpin* (1539).
    (4) 'Yangguan sandie', *Zhongxin zhenzhuan* (1585).
    (5) 'Yangguan sandie', *Tōkō-kin-pu* (eighteenth century).

Example 7. Various versions of 'Yangguan sandie' (cf. Example 1)

(1) 渭城朝雨浥輕塵　　　客舍青青柳色新

(2) 長亭柳陰陰　　　渭城朝雨浥輕塵　　　客舍青青　　柳色新

(3) 渭城朝雨浥輕塵　　　客舍　青青柳色新

(4) 渭城朝雨輕塵　　　客舍青青柳色新

(5) 長亭柳依依　渭城朝雨浥輕塵　　客舍青青　　柳色新

勸君更盡一盃酒　　西出　陽關的那無故人　　etc.

勸君更盡一盃酒　　西出陽關無故人　　etc.

須憶重遷當遂志　莫因此別　便傷神　前程万里鯤　鵬運

勸君更盡一盃酒　　西出陽關無故人　　etc.

勸君更盡一盃酒　　西出陽關　無故人　　etc.

名位　三台鵷鷥神　　勸君更盡一盃酒　　西出陽關　無故人

Table 2

| Text: | 勸 | 君 | 更 | 盡 | 一 | 杯 | 酒 | |
|---|---|---|---|---|---|---|---|---|
| Notation: { | 茜 | 四 | 笃 | 茜 | 三 | 笃 | 茜 | *Tōkō-kin-pu* (jiliang diao) |
| | 茜 | 四 | 笃 | 茜 | 三 | 笃 | 茜 | *Qinxue rumen* (wushi jun) |
| Notes: | B♭ | G | (G) | G | F | (G) | G | |

In *Tōkō-kin-pu* the significance of the mode, diaoyi, which was important in the Ming dynasty, is completely lost.

In the Ming dynasty the tunings were much more closely connected with the melodies, but such an irregular note as E♭ in jiliang diao sounds unnatural in the melodic structure. Therefore, after the middle of the Qing dynasty irregular tunings and melodies came to be adjusted and arranged according to the system of five authentic modes.

In the modern repertoire of qin music, however, the tonal or melodic structure still has a strong relationship to the tuning. Melodies can be freely developed with delicate ornaments, but most qin pieces possess common melodic features especially at the beginning and end. A qin piece begins with such melodic features as follows:

(a) The first phrase, in many cases, is an ascending melody indicating successively the notes of the tuning.

(b) A melodic pattern, including glissando based on the notes of the tuning.

(c) The 'keynote' of the piece, which is indicated under the title of each piece,[8] is emphasised at the end of the first phrase.

Melodies develop in the middle of a piece, and some typical melodic patterns can be repeated in modified or varied forms. For instance, in the first section of 'Yangguan sandie' (see Example 1), the phrases 2(=5) and 6(=8) are repeated, and some phrases of the first section also appear

Example 8. Opening phrases[9]

8   The 'key-note' is not necessarily coincident with the fundamental note of the mode.
9   (1) 'Zhangmen yuan', *Meian qin pu* (1931).
   (2) 'Yangguan sandie', *Qinxue rumen* (1864).
   The sign * denotes the 'key-note'.

in the second and third sections in modified forms. Sometimes intervals of a fourth, fifth or sixth appear, but qin music mainly consists of flowing ascending and descending melodies using successive major seconds and minor thirds, and melodic patterns in a narrow compass produced by the portamento technique.

Many qin pieces end with the special cadential formulae or weisheng, a coda, in which the characteristics of the mode or tuning are indicated (see p. 135). The last phrase is usually completed with a tonal pattern of octaves emphasising the final note (see Example 9).

Example 9. Closing phrases[10]

As discussed above, the tunings and melodies of qin music have gradually changed during its long history. Yet the tunings or modes still have a close relationship to the melodies, though they do not affect them so strongly as they did in the Ming dynasty: the characteristics of a tuning are emphasised at the beginning and end of each piece, and the key-note of each piece is effectively indicated. This is why the key-note is almost always written under the title of the piece, for example 'zhonglü jun *gongyin*' or 'wushi jun *shangyin*'.[11]

The metre and the rhythm also have an essential function in the melodies of qin music. It is a unique characteristic of qin music that the metre and rhythm are left to the interpretation of the individual performer. The difference of metrical or rhythmic interpretation can produce a different melodic atmosphere. This is probably why qin music was able to survive during its long history, and retained its artistic vigour.

10   Sources as in note 9.
11   See note 8.

## Bibliography

### Books and articles

*Guangling san* 廣陵散, ed. Zhongyang yinyue xueyuan minzu yinyue yanjiu suo,中央音樂學院民族音樂研究所, Yinyue chubanshe音樂出版社, Peking 1958

*Guqin quji,* 古琴曲集, I. Zhongyang yinyue xueyuan, Zhongguo yinyue yanjiu suo 中央音樂學院中國音樂研究所, Peking 1962

Kaufmann, W., *Musical notations of the orient*, I, Bloomington, Indiana, 1967

Liang Ming-Yueh, 'A study of tiao-i, "the meaning of the mode" ', *Perspectives in Asian Music: essays in honor of Dr Laurence E.R. Picken, Asian Music* VI, nos. 1−2, New York 1975

Lieberman, F., 'Texted tunes in the Mei-an Chih-Pin', *Perspectives in Asian Music: essays in honor of Dr Laurence E.R. Picken, Asian Music* VI, nos. 1−2, New York 1975

Lui Tsun-yuen呂振原, 'Ch'in techniques of the right hand', *Selected Reports in Ethnomusicology* I no. 2, Los Angeles, 1966

Mitani, Y., 'Chūgoku kin no kifu-hö'中國琴の記譜法, *Transonic* no. 2, Zen-on Gakufu Shuppan-sha, 1974

Picken, L.E.R. 'A twelfth-century secular Chinese song in zither-tablature', *Asia Major*, 16(1−2), 1971.

Shen Zaonong 沈草農, Zha Fuxi查阜西, Zhang Ziqian 張子謙, *Guqin chujie,* 古琴初階, Yinyue chubanshe音樂出版社, Peking 1961

van Gulik, R.H., *The Lore of the Chinese Lute*, Monumenta Nipponica Monographs, Tokyo 1939

Wang Guangqi王光祈, *Fanyi qin pu zhi yanjiu* 翻譯琴譜之研究, Shanghai 1931

Yang Yinliu 楊蔭瀏, 'Dui guqin "Yanguan sandie" de chubu de yanjiu' 對古琴曲陽關三疊的初步的研究, in *Minzu yinyue lunwen ji*民族音樂論文集 I, 1956

Yang Yinliu and Hou Zuowu 侯作吾, *Guqin qu huibian*古琴曲彙編, Yinyue chubanshe, Peking 1956

Yang Yinliu and Yin Falu 陰法魯, *Song Jiang Baishi chuangzuo gequ yanjiu*宋姜白石創作歌曲研究, Yinyue chubanshe, Peking 1957


### Qin handbooks

*Faming qin pu* 發明琴譜, ed. by Huang Lonshan 黃龍山, 1530, contained in *Qinqu jicheng*

*Fengxuan xuanpin* 風宣玄品, ed. Zhu Houjue朱厚爝, 1539, contained in *Qinqu jicheng*

*Meian qin pu*梅庵琴譜, ed. Xu Zhuo徐卓, 1931

*Shenji bipu* 神奇秘譜, ed. Zhu Quan 朱權, 1425, contained in *Qinqu jicheng*

*Shilin guangji*事林廣記, ed. Chen Yuanjing 陳元靚, 1269, contained in *Qinqu jicheng*

*Taigu yiyin*太古遺音, or *Taiyin da quanji*太音大全集, ed. Zhu Quan, 1413, contained in *Qinqu jicheng*

*Tianwenge qin pu jicheng*天聞閣琴譜集成, ed. Tang Yiming唐彝銘, 1876

*Tōkō-kin-pu*東皋琴譜, ed. Sigiura Kinzen 杉浦琴川, early eighteenth century, 1865 edition; also ed. Suzuki Ryu 鈴木龍, 1771

*Qinqu jicheng*琴曲集成, I, 1, ed. Zhongyang yinyue xueyuan zhongguo yinyue yanjiu suo 中央音樂學院中國音樂研究所, Beijing guqin yanjiu hui北京古琴研究會, Zhonghua shuju中華書局, Peking 1963

*Qinxue rumen*琴學入門, ed. Zhang He 張鶴, 1864

*Zheyin shizi qin pu* 浙音釋字琴譜, ed. Long Jing 龔經, before 1491, contained in *Qinqu jicheng*

*Zhongxin zhenzhuan*重脩真傳, ed. Yang Biaozheng楊表正, 1585

*Ziyuantang qin pu* 自遠堂琴譜, ed. Wu Hong 吳虹, 1802

**Glossary**

cilong 側弄
cishang diao 側商調
'Changhong' 長虹
da yuan 打圓
diaoyi 調意
'Fanu' 發怒
fanyin 泛音
fu 拂
'Gaoshan liushui' 高山流水
Guan Pinghu 管平湖
'Guangling san' 廣陵散
'Guyuan' 古怨
Hou Zuowu 侯作吾
huangzhong diao 黃鐘調
huangzhong jun 黃鐘均
Jiang Kui 姜夔
jianzi pu 減字譜
jiazhong jun 夾鐘均
'Jieshi diao yulan' 碣石調幽蘭
jiliang diao 淒涼調
kun 滾
linzhong diao 林鐘調
manshang diao 慢商調
'Oulu wangji' 鷗鷺忘機
qin (ch'in) 琴
qindao 琴道
ruibin diao 蕤賓調
taicu diao 太簇調
wai diao 外調
Wang Wei 王維
weisheng 尾聲
wushi diao 無射調
wushi jun 無射均
Xi Kang 嵇康
Xia Yifeng 夏一峯
'Yangguan qu' 陽關曲
'Yangguan sandie' 陽關三疊
yici jun 夷則均

Zha Fuxi 查阜西
Zhang Shibin 張世彬
'Zhangmen yuan' 長門怨
zhengdiao 正調
zhenglong 正弄
zhonglü jun 仲呂均
zhonglü diao 仲呂調

# Aspects of form in North Indian ālāp and dhrupad

RICHARD WIDDESS

I. Introduction
II. Rāgālāp
    (a) Modern performance
    (b) Śārṅgadeva's description
    (c) Conclusions
III. The dhrupad composition
    (a) Tāla
    (b) Melodic structure
    (c) 'Dhrupad/kīrtana form' and *dhruva-prabandha*
IV. Nom tom and bāṃt
V. Conclusions
    Appendix: Additional evidence for the form of dhruva-prabandha

## I. Introduction

*Dhrupad*, from the Sanskrit *dhruva* ('fixed', hence 'refrain') and *pada* ('verse'), denotes a short poem with musical setting, in four or two lines that include a refrain, usually written in the Braj dialect of Hindi on religious themes. In the North Indian tradition of art-music, a large repertory of such songs is preserved,[1] each of which can serve as the basis for extended development (largely improvised) of the appropriate *rāga* (melody-type) and *tāla* (rhythmic pattern). In many

I should like to thank Śrī T.L. Rāna, Pandit Sīyārām Tiwārī, Śrī Vijay Kichlū, Mr William Coates, Dr R.S. McGregor, Dr J.D. Smith and Dr E. te Nijenhuis for providing and helping me to understand the materials presented in this essay, and especially my supervisor, Dr L.E.R. Picken, for his constant inspiration and guidance.

1  Primarily through oral tradition. For recently published collections of dhrupad compositions with musical notation, see Bhātkhande, *Kramik pustak mālikā* (1954–9) (hereafter cited as *KPM*) and Rājā Nawāb Āli Khān, *Mariphunnagmāt* (1952) (hereafter *MN*). A seventeenth-century anthology of dhrupad texts attributed to Baiju Baksu has been edited and published by Śarmā (1972). No dhrupad compositions from before the nineteenth century have so far come to light with contemporary musical notation.

aspects of technique and form, the performance of dhrupad differs from that of *khyāl*, now the more prominent genre of North Indian vocal music.[2] A distinguishing feature of dhrupad is the long, improvised modal prelude in free tempo, called *ālāp*, which normally precedes performance of the dhrupad composition itself; this introductory ālāp is also found in instrumental music.

The art of dhrupad-performance is preserved only in the most conservative and intellectual schools, and is relatively unfamiliar even to Indian audiences. It is regarded, however, as the oldest and most prestigious genre of North Indian music. The tradition that dhrupad derives from the ancient music of the Vedic hymns (composed in the second millenium B.C.) may be discounted as merely an expression of venerability; but there is more reason to suppose, as is often claimed, that it maintains a tradition of Hindu—Moslem court music which flourished under Mān Siṅgh of Gwalior (1486—1525), Akbār the Great (1556—1605), and many other sixteenth- and seventeenth-century rulers, before the rise to pre-eminence of khyāl in the eighteenth century.

The purpose of this article is to determine whether there is internal, musical evidence for the antiquity or otherwise of the dhrupad tradition. In view of the wide variation in form, technique and style between schools and between individual performers of dhrupad, our attention is engaged principally by those aspects of form that are relatively constant: in particular, by the dhrupad songs themselves, and by the *rāgālāp*, or first part of the improvised modal prelude, during which the characteristics of the rāga are systematically set out. Each of these is analysed in some detail, with reference to specific examples in transcription. For evidence of parallel musical forms, reference is made to other contemporary genres of North and South Indian music, and to a thirteenth-century Sanskrit text, the *Saṅgītaratnākara* of Śārṅgadeva (henceforth *SSR*), which is the most detailed source of textual information about early Indian musical forms.

The musical objects in singing dhrupad are exposition and development of the rāga, expressive rendition of the composed text and melody, and demonstration of the melodic sensitivity, rhythmic dexterity and vocal technique of the singer. Dhrupad is therefore normally performed by a soloist, or by two singers at the most (who improvise alternately and combine in performance of the composed song). A solo melodic instrument (traditionally the vīna or sāraṅgī, now frequently the harmonium) may also participate in a subordinate capacity. Essential accompaniment is provided by the tambūrā, a large, fretless long lute, the open strings of which are gently agitated to provide a continuous, humming drone throughout the performance; and the mṛdaṅg or pakhāvaj, a horizontal barrel-drum resembling the South Indian mṛdaṅgam but somewhat larger and deeper-toned. The use of the native pakhāvaj, whose rôle is second only to that of the soloist in importance, distinguishes dhrupad from the majority of other North Indian genres, in which the use of the pair of small kettle-drums called tablā suggests Middle Eastern influence.

The opening ālāp comprises two stages: the rāgālāp, in which the rāga is gradually unfolded in lower, middle and upper octaves in free tempo; and the *nom tom*, in which a rhythmic pulse

2   For a detailed study of khyāl see Wade 1971.

is introduced.[3] There is no text, but various meaningless syllables are used as an aid to articulation. The whole ālāp is performed without the participation of the drum.

On completion of the ālāp, the soloist sings the dhrupad composition (*bandiś* or *cīz*) in slow or medium tempo, and is now joined by the drum player, who improvises within the limits of the tāla to which the song is set. The composition may have four sections (*pada*), called *sthāyī*, *antarā*, *samcārī* and *ābhog*, or alternatively only the first two sections. On completion of the composition, repetitions of the first section (*sthāyī*) are interspersed with variations or 'divisions' (*bāṃṭ*), partly improvised, in which the words and melody of the composition are sung in strict diminution (*lay-bāṃṭ*), or the words set to new melodic phrases that are in cross-rhythm against the tāla (*bol-bāṃṭ*).

In structure, the performance of dhrupad closely resembles that of *kīrtana* or *kriti*, the principal genre of South Indian vocal music. The following table sets out the principal sections of a dhrupad performance under the headings 'improvised' and 'composed', and places these in parallel with the corresponding sections of an extended kriti performance.

| dhrupad | | kriti | |
|---|---|---|---|
| improvised sections | composed sections | improvised sections | composed sections |
| 1 rāgālāp | | 1 rāgālāpanam | |
| 2 nom tom | | 2 tānam | |
| | 3    dhrupad: | | 3    kriti: |
| | a) sthāyī | | a)    pallavī |
| | b) antarā | | b)    anupallavī |
| | c) samcārī | | c) ⎱ |
| | d) ābhog | | d) ⎰ caraṇam |
| | 4    lay-bāṃṭ | | 4    anuloma |
| 5 bol-bāṃṭ | | 5 niraval | |

The forms associated with dhrupad and kīrtana/kriti are compared in more detail later in this study (pp. 164 and 167); but the whole relationship, musical and historical, between these two genres is a matter for further investigation.

## II. Rāgālāp

### (a) Modern performance

Ālāp is 'a kind of improvised prelude in free time in which the melodic characteristics of the rāg being performed are clearly established and developed' (Jairazbhoy 1971: 28f), in which

---

3    The rāgālāp is more often termed *vilambit* (slow) ālāp, and successively faster sections of nom tom are called *madhya* (moderate) and *drut* (quick) ālāp. However, this terminology is in some respects misleading, (a) because the distinction between rāgālāp and nom tom is between tempo rubato and tempo giusto, and between vocal and instrumental style (see p. 00), rather than between slow and faster speeds; and (b) because the nom tom may itself comprise sections in slow, medium and fast speeds.

'the singer rehearses the essential traits of the rāga in question, its scale, the notes particularly stressed, the appropriate ornaments' (Sachs 1944: 191), and thereby 'prepares the foundation of the prevailing *rasa* (ethos)' (Kaufmann 1968: 25). This is often the most extended part of a dhrupad performance, since it is here that the performer has the maximum freedom to improvise on the melodic materials of the rāga. Members of the Ḍāgar family and their disciples are particularly noted for their extended ālāps, which sometimes last thirty minutes or more.[4]

In ālāp the performer is bound by few if any 'rules' regarding the form of his improvisation or the technique to be adopted. However, in rāgālāp (the first of the two principal sections of ālāp) the same procedure is followed, more or less closely, by many performers. For the purposes of analysis, therefore, we take two examples in which this 'standard procedure' is clearly demonstrated.

Example 10 (p. 168) is a short 'student's ālāp' in rāg Bhairav, as taught in 1954 to Mr William Coates by Dr Suresh Chandra Chakkravarti of Calcutta, a dilrubā player and musicologist. This example is of interest because it represents an attempt by a practising musician to convey to a pupil the essential form and technique of ālāp-improvisation, and because it demonstrates the similarity between instrumental and vocal ālāp.[5] Example 11 (p. 170) shows the rāgālāp from a performance of dhrupad in rāg Bāgeśrī, by Śrī T.L. Rāna (recorded by the author at Banaras, February 1976).

In the analysis of these examples, it will not be possible to discuss the structure of individual rāgas, since we are concerned only with those aspects of formal organisation that are the same for all rāgas. The notes of the scale, referred to in Indian terminology by the syllables *sa, ri, ga, ma, pa, dha, ni*, will be represented in the discussion by the numbers 1 to 7 respectively. Different octaves are distinguished as follows: lower octave: $\underline{1}$–$\underline{7}$; middle octave: 1–7; upper octave: $\dot{1}$–$\dot{7}$. In the musical examples, the notes sa to ni are represented by the pitches C to B respectively, except where otherwise stated.

The basis of the modern North Indian rāga is a scale of five or more notes, of which the first (sa) functions as a ground-note or tonic, and is sustained throughout the performance as a drone (together with the fifth or fourth). Since rāgālāp is an exposition of the characteristics of the rāga, the first step is therefore to establish the tonic, and it is from this note, or with a phrase leading to this note, that the improvisation begins (see Examples 10 and 11 below, *ad initium*).

The development proceeds in a number of sections, each of which concludes with a return to the tonic. Each section ends with a cadential formula called *mukhṛā*, the form of which varies according to the melodic characteristics of the rāga; in Examples 10 and 11 the mukhṛā takes the forms shown in Example 1.

The tonic therefore plays an important part in the structure of rāgālāp, as initial, final, and sectional final. Intervening sections of melodic development are heard against the background of the sustained tonic drone of the tambūrā, with which each note forms a consonant or dis-

---

4   Comparatively short ālāps may be heard on the Bärenreiter recordings BM 30 L 2018 and BM 30 SL 2051.
5   I am indebted to Mr Coates for allowing me to use his *sārgam* notation of this ālāp, which I have transcribed into staff notation.

Example 1

sonant relationship (Jairazbhoy 1971: 65ff). The relationship of the 'strong' (*vādī*) note or notes of the rāga with the tonic is particularly important in determining the quasi-emotional 'flavour' (rasa) of the rāga.

Within each section, the melody rises or falls a certain distance above or below the tonic and returns to it. At or near the beginning of the rāgālāp the materials of the rāga are briefly stated in the lower octave. However, the systematic exposition of the rāga in the middle octave, which follows, constitutes the main interest in rāgālāp. In this process, which has been outlined by Jairazbhoy (1961), each note of the ascending scale (if present in the rāga) is introduced in turn, and developed in combination with notes previously heard; thus the range of the melody gradually expands. In extended performances, a whole section (or several sections) may be devoted to the development of each note; the introduction of more than one new note in a single section leads to a more rapid development. When the octave above the tonic has been reached, the performer usually introduces notes of the upper octave in a single section. A final return to the tonic and mukhṛā then brings the whole rāgālāp to a close, and in dhrupad the performer proceeds to the nom tom (see p. 167).

The range and emphasised notes of each section in Examples 10 and 11 are shown in Example 2. During development of the middle octave, the shape of the melody within each sec-

Example 2

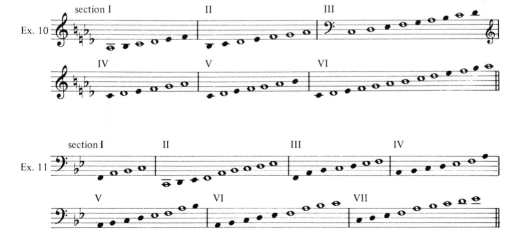

tion is that of an arch or series of arches, rising from the region of the tonic towards a peak in the region of the note to be emphasised, and falling again to the tonic. The highest note of the 'arch' is not necessarily the note most emphasised, for higher notes than this may be touched lightly, or merely suggested in ornamentation, before being firmly established in subsequent sections.

Regarding the development of the melody from phrase to phrase within each section of the rāgālāp, Jairazbhoy suggests (1961) that a quasi-mathematical technique of note-permutation called *svaraprastāra* has an important part to play. This technique is first described by the eighth-century author Mataṅga (*Bṛhaddeśī* – 1928: 37) in its simplest form, that of a scale-exercise called *prastāra alaṃkāra*, of which he provides a specimen in notation (*ibid.*: 37 and 47f) – Example 3. The example shows alternate ascending and descending scale-segments of increasing length, beginning and ending on the same note.

Example 3

The more complex svaraprastāra, which is first described by Śārṅgadeva (*SSR* I.4.62–70) in the thirteenth century and is still practised as an exercise today, includes, between each ascending note-sequence and the following descending sequence, all possible permutations of the notes of the sequence, so arranged as to make a logical progression from first to last. Thus instead of, for example, 1 2 3, 3 2 1 (the second sequence of Mataṅga's example), we find: 1 2 3, 2 1 3, 1 3 2, 3 1 2, 2 3 1, 3 2 1 (for a full account see Jairazbhoy 1961).

Example 3 might easily be taken for a schematic outline of modern rāgālāp, which may therefore have its remote origins in a simple scale-exercise of considerable antiquity. In view of this resemblance, Jairazbhoy suggests that the systematic permutation of notes in Śārṅgadeva's svaraprastāra is in some way analogous to the phrase-by-phrase development of the melody in rāgālāp. However, although this analogy is supported by a passage from Bhātkhaṇḍe's *Saṅgītaśāstra*, its relevance to actual examples of rāgālāp is not shown; Jairazbhoy concedes that 'of the several aspects of the svarapastāra, the extension of the notes of the scale is perhaps the most important in this context'. It may be doubted whether note-permutation as such is widely used in rāgālāp. It is unlikely that a mathematical ordering of permutations would commend itself at the moment of performance to a creative musician; and in any case, as Bhātkhaṇḍe admits, not all permutations of a particular sequence of notes would necessarily be compatible with the melodic dynamics of the rāga being performed: 'Only those [notes, permutations] should be used that are acceptable in the rāga being manifested' (quoted in Jairazbhoy 1961). It might be argued that the 'performance rules' of most rāgas and the preference for stepwise movement in Indian melody leave only limited scope for note-permutation. If neither the mathematical ordering nor the completeness of the series of permutations is important, one must conclude either that the sequence of notes and phrases in rāgālāp is somewhat arbitrary, or else that some other principle is at work.

Examination of Examples 10 and 11 suggests that note-permutation is not a feature of these examples, but that each phrase is closely related, either by repetition or by expansion, to what has gone before. We therefore use the following method to show the relationship of parts to the whole. Each melodic phrase (or group of phrases) is written in cipher notation on a separate horizontal line. Immediate repetition of a note and precise rhythmic values are not indicated: a circle round a figure denotes a note longer than the other notes of the same phrase. Ornamentation, indicated by grace-notes in the transcriptions, is also omitted (parentheses enclose other notes that are considered to be primarily ornamental in function). The end of each phrase (corresponding in performance to a pause) is marked ’.

Successive phrases are so disposed on the page that if a phrase or part of a phrase is repeated, the repeated material is located vertically beneath the original, as at (a) below. If the repetition introduces new material, the new material is distinguished by the sign ⌐ (b). However, an exception to the procedure of vertical alignment occurs when new material is introduced in the middle of a phrase. In this case, the vertical alignment with previous phrases is disturbed, as indicated by the arrows (c).

(a) 1    2    3’
         2    3’

(b) 1    2    3’
         2    3   ⌐4’

(c)

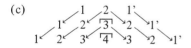

Experiment shows that while this method can be applied in the analysis of samples of rāgālāp, it cannot be used where any re-ordering of notes takes place, as in svaraprastāra. For example, the permutations 1 2 3, 2 1 3, 1 3 2 etc. (given on p. 148) cannot be aligned in the manner of (a), (b) or (c).

Figure 1 shows an analysis of Example 10 using the method described (the development of the lower octave in section III is omitted in the analysis). Two immediate observations may be made:

(1) Every phrase can be related to previous phrases in the manner of (a), (b) or (c) above.

(2) The principal method of development is that shown at (c) above. Here a rising and falling phrase is expanded at successive repetitions, by adding higher and higher notes at the apex. The operation of this procedure, which we term ‘internal scalar expansion’, can be seen at a glance from Figure 1, where the introduction of each successively higher note is aligned beneath the sign †. Arrows radiating to right and left of this column reflect the gradual expansion in range of successive phrases.

Figure 1

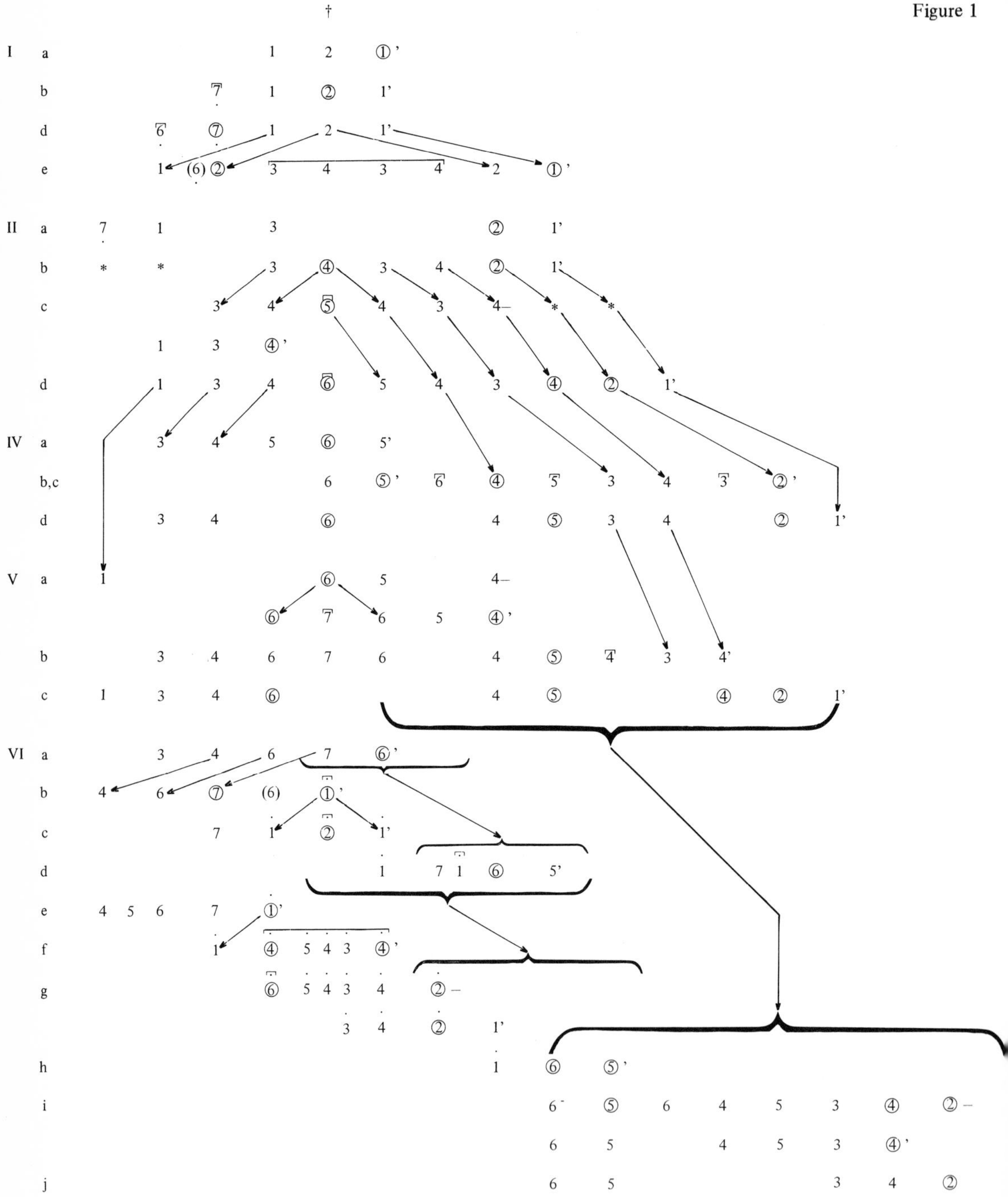

Section I, phrase C, and section III omitted.
Note: the introduction of each successively higher note is aligned beneath the sign †.

Figure 1 therefore supports our view that the phrase-by-phrase development in rāgālāp is a logical process, and that the principle of range-expansion operates at the level of individual phrases, as well as in the organisation of the whole.

Let us examine parts of Figure 1 in more detail. The opening section establishes the tonic and the second degree (one of the vādi or stressed notes of the rāga). The two notes are combined at the outset in a rising and falling motif: 1 2 1. This motif is then approached from below, bringing in the lower notes 7 and 6 (phrase c initiates the development *below* the tonic which is continued in section III, and is therefore omitted in this analysis). In the final phrase, the motif is expanded to include notes 3 and 4.

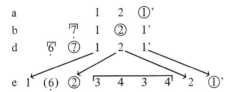

Phrase e is a particularly clear example of 'internal expansion'. In Example 10, the note 2 is normally used only in descent, and omitted in ascent. The ascending step 2 3 in phrase e is therefore unusual, and indicates that the notes 3 4 3 4 are but an interpolation into the basic motif 1 2 1.

In section II, the notes 4, 5 and 6 are introduced and developed, although it is 4 that is particularly stressed (cf. p. 148). The original motif 1 2 1 is further expanded, in several stages, from 7 1 3 2 1 (phrase a) to 1 3 4 6 5 4 3 4 2 1 (phrase d). Notes 2 and 5 are omitted in ascending phrases, and 3 in descending phrases; these features, and the 'crooked' (*vakra*) descending line 4 3 4 2 1, take precedence over regular scale-order. Thus the 'method' is modified to reflect the characteristics of the rāga concerned. As higher notes are introduced, the lower notes tend to be omitted (see the instances marked * in Figure 1); this tendency continues in later sections (where it is not specially marked in Figure 1).

In sections IV and V the notes 5, 6 and 7 are developed in a similar manner to that described. Section VI is the last section, in which the octave of the tonic is reached, and notes of the upper octave introduced; the total range of the melody is considerably greater here than in any previous section. Accordingly, we find that a somewhat different procedure is adopted. First, the ascent to the upper tonic, from 3 to 1̇, is developed in phrases a, b and e; then the region of the upper tonic and notes of the upper octave are developed in phrases c, f and g; and finally the descent to the tonic is effected in phrases d, h, i and j. We should therefore distinguish two types of phrase-by-phrase development, represented diagramatically below. In the earlier stages of the rāgālāp, each phrase may comprise an ascent and descent, rising from and returning to the region of the tonic (a). As the total range of the melody expands, however, the ascending line, the apex, and the descending line may each be developed separately (b).

(a)   (b)

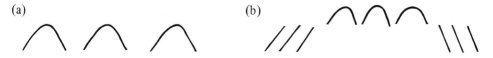

Figure 2

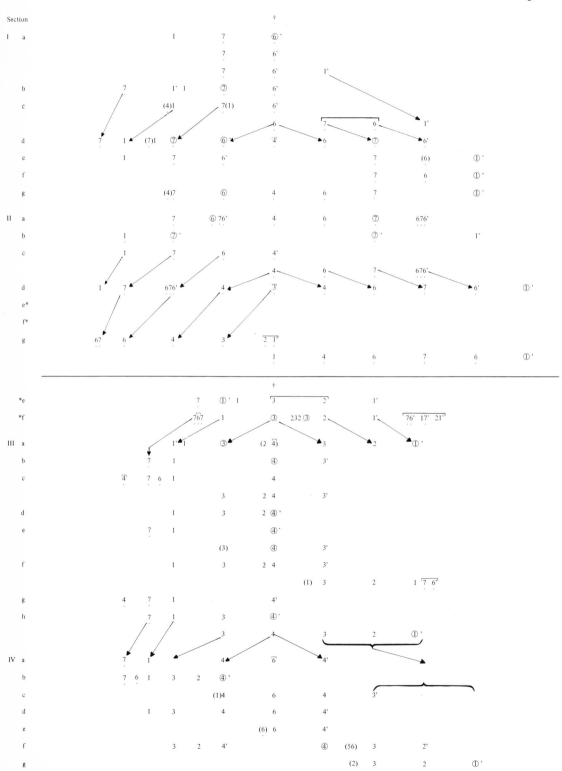

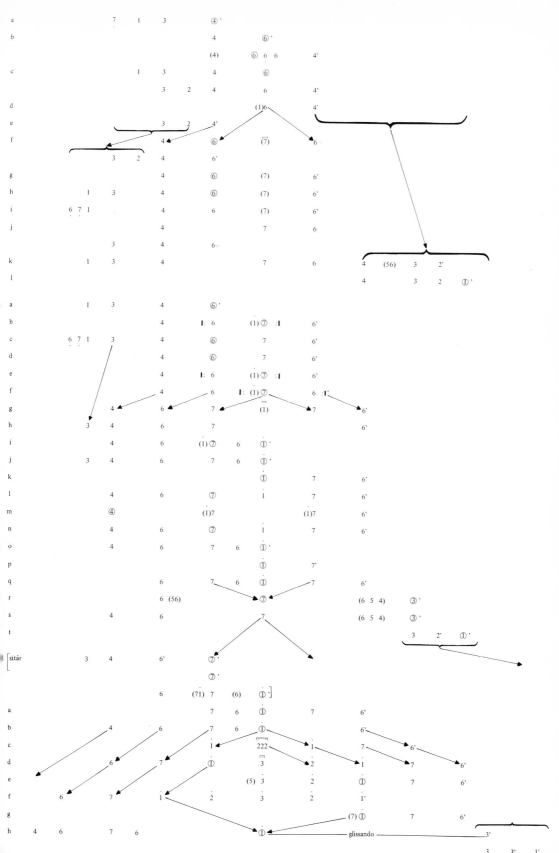

I denotes repetition of the notes enclosed

A feature of the musical development that is not shown in Figure 1 is the variety of treatment given to repeated phrases and notes. Thus the note 2 occurs five times in section I. Reference to the transcription shows that this note is differently rendered on each occurrence:

(1) phrase a: short, repeated;

(2) phrase b: prolonged, not repeated, approached glissando from below;

(3) phrase d: short, repeated, approached glissando from above;

(4) phrase e: prolonged, repeated short, approached glissando from below;

(5) phrase e: short, not repeated, approached glissando from above, vibrato.

Thus the repetition of material gives scope for subtle variation of emphasis and articulation, an aspect of the performance that often cannot be adequately conveyed in notation.

The 'student's ālāp' that we have analysed is a short example of a form that in the context of actual performance might occupy some ten or twenty minutes. It might be argued that the greater length of rāgālāp in performance is achieved by free note-permutation on the svaraprastāra model, within the framework demonstrated by the 'student's ālāp'. It might alternatively be the case that no additional procedure of development is introduced, but that the varied repetition of material, as seen above, is alone responsible for greater length.

Example 11, the rāgālāp from a dhrupad performance in rāg Bāgeśrī, supports the second hypothesis. An analysis of this example using the same method as Figure 1 is set out in Figure 2. Again, every phrase can be placed in alignment with previous phrases, and the principal method of development is by 'internal scalar expansion'. However, there is considerably more repetition of individual phrases than in the 'student's ālāp'. Again, each time that a particular phrase is repeated, there is some change in articulation or emphasis.

An important aspect of this performance is the choice of notes on which phrases end. Such notes are determined by the structure of the rāga: only the 'strong' notes of the rāga (1, 3, 4 and 6) occur as the final note of a phrase, while this function is performed rarely by 2, and never by 5 and 7, since they are 'weak' notes.[6] Each time that a new note is introduced in Example 11, it occurs first in the middle of a phrase, owing to the procedure of internal scalar expansion (see Figure 2: section III a; IV a; V f; VI g). Often the note is only lightly touched at this stage.

Example 4

6   The parallel with the melodies of the seventh-century Kuḍumiyāmalai Inscription (Widdess: in press) is striking.

If the note is a 'strong' note of the rāga, the next step is to establish it as the final note of a phrase (III d; V f; VI i). In this process it may be necessary to repeat material several times, gradually transferring emphasis from the original final note to the new final note (Example 4: for the special symbols used here, cf. p. 168). Thus repetition of material may be used in order to establish a new note as the final note of a phrase.

A second function of repetition is to delay a climax. In the present example, this device is used to delay the central climax of the whole rāgālāp, the ascent to the upper tonic (Example 5). This note is first suggested (through a process of internal scalar expansion) in section VI, phrase b. The next step, therefore, is to establish this note firmly by taking it as the final note of a phrase. However, in c, the singer returns to an earlier stage in the development (cf. section V, phrase i), in which the upper tonic is not even suggested. He then gradually re-introduces this note in phrases d to h, which are all varied repetitions of the motif 4 6 7 6. Finally the tonic is established firmly at the end of phrase i. (Here again, movement characteristic of the rāga – 6 7 6 1̇ – replaces scale order.) To emphasise the climax further, the material of phrases e to i is repeated in phrases l to o.

Example 5

Example 11 shows that the techniques of development exhibited in the instrumental 'student's ālāp' (Example 10) are also to be found in vocal ālāp as performed in the dhrupad tradition, where greater length is attained by extensive repetition and variation of material. While a performer's improvisation in rāgālāp is limited, in principle, only by the structure and 'performance rules' of the rāga, it is clear that the technique of internal scalar expansion provides a means of extended melodic development, and can be adapted to reflect the characteristics of individual rāgas.

### (b) Śārṅgadeva's description

Evidence for the antiquity of the technique and form of modern rāgālāp is to be found in the thirteenth-century *Saṅgītaratnākara* of Śārṅgadeva. The following extract is the earliest known description of the formal structure of rāgālāp, or *rāgālapti* as it is called in this source. The following technical terms are used.

(1)    *sthāyī:* defined as 'the note on which the rāga is established' (*yatropaveśyate rāgaḥ svare*), this note functions as initial, sectional final, and final, and is therefore translated 'tonic'. The term should not be confused with the modern sthāyi or first section of the dhrupad composition (see p. 161).

(2)    *dvyardha:* the fourth note, counting from and including the tonic, i.e. the fourth scale-degree; translated 'the fourth'.

(3)    *dviguṇa:* the eighth note from the tonic, i.e. the upper tonic; translated 'the octave'.

(4)    *ardhasthita:* a note or notes between the fourth and the upper tonic; translated 'intervening note(s)'.

Śārṅgadeva's description (III.189b–96) runs as follows:[7]

189b    *Rāgālāpana* or *ālapti* is considered to be a demonstration [of the rāga].

190    It is said to be of two kinds by reason of the distinction between rāga and composition. *Rāgālapti* is that which is not connected with a composition.[8]

191    It [rāgālapti] should have four sections: thus the skilled in song know it. The note on which the rāga is established is called the tonic [*sthāyī*].

192    The fourth note from this should be [called] *dvyardha.* There should be a phrase (*calanam*, lit. 'movement') called 'opening phrase' (*mukhacāla*) about a note lower than this [the fourth]. This is the first section.

193    Having made a phrase about the fourth, [there should be] a cadence. This is the second section. The eighth note from the tonic is called the octave (*dviguṇa*).

194    The notes between the fourth and the octave are called intervening notes (*ardhasthita*). Having made a phrase about an intervening note [there should be] a cadence. [This is] the third section.

195    Having made a phrase about the octave [there should be] a cadence on the tonic. [This is] the fourth section. Rāgālapti is held by the worthy to have these four sections.

196    The establishment of the rāga should be effected by means of very gradual, clear, circuitous ornamentations [*sthāya*],[9] and should be pervaded by the vital notes (*jīvasvara*) [of the rāga].

It is clear from this account that the gradual extension of range, from the region of the tonic to the octave above, in a number of sections each cadencing on the lower tonic, was the most prominent feature of rāgālapti, as it is of rāgālāp. In the four sections of rāgālapti, the melodic development took place below the fourth, around the fourth, between the fourth and the upper tonic, and around the upper tonic respectively. Today a greater or smaller number of sections

7    I am grateful to Dr J.D. Smith for invaluable assistance in preparing all the translations from Sanskrit in this article.

8    Śārṅgadeva appears to use the term *ālapti* in the general sense of 'improvisation'; improvisation based on a composition (*rupakālapti*) is described in *SSR* III. 197–202.

9    For the *sthāyas* see *SSR* III. 97–189.

might be used, and the lower and upper octaves would also be briefly explored; but the emphasis is still on the gradual development of the ascending scale in the middle octave.

Śārṅgadeva stresses the importance of ornamentation (*sthāya*) and of the 'strong' notes of the rāga (*jīvasvara*), but does not describe how, in practice, the melody should evolve from phrase to phrase. However, in a later chapter (VI. 328–99 and 669–779), the same author gives detailed instructions for playing rāgālapti in various specific rāgas, on the principal melodic instruments of the day: the kinnari vīṇā (a fretted stick-zither) and the transverse bamboo flute (vaṃśa). The most explicit of these instructions (VI. 669–76) describe the playing of rāgālapti in rāga Madhyamādi on the flute:

> 669b/670    When, having played [the note] Madhyama as tonic, the third note is played vibrato (*kampita*), the second [is played] slowly, and a cadence made on the tonic, then that is said by the wise to be the first section of Madhyamādi [rāga].
>
> 671    When, having played the third note vibrato, the fourth above and then the fifth, the fourth and the second, [there is] a cadence on the initial,
>
> 672/3    then [that] is called the second section by Śārṅgadeva. When, having played the fourth note with a shake (*āhatya*), the tonic and the note above it together [quickly] (*samuccārya*), the fourth and fifth slowly, the sixth and fifth, and the second, [there is] a cadence on the initial,
>
> 674    then the experts say that it is the third section. Having played the initial, the second and the fourth, then the fifth [and] seventh,
>
> 675    and having played the eighth note slowly, the second, then the note above that, the second, the seventh, the fifth, the fourth,
>
> 676    and the second, [there should be] a cadence on the initial; [thus] the fourth section is prescribed.

A realisation of these instructions is attempted in Example 6. The note Madhyama, the tonic, is equated with *c'*, to facilitate comparison with other examples in this study. It is possible that a major seventh and augmented fourth (*antara* ga and *kākali* ni) would have been used in ascending phrases.

Further instructions are given for playing rāgālapti in thirty-one additional rāgas on the flute, and in twenty-three of the same rāgas on the vīṇā. In most cases, detailed instructions are given

Example 6

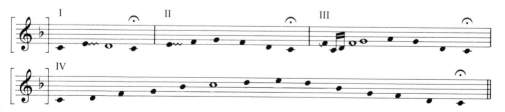

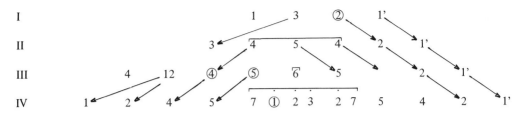

Figure 3

for the first section only. In a general statement, however, it is made clear that the step-by-step expansion of range described in chapter III, and demonstrated in the case of rāga Madhyamādi, is to be applied in all rāgas:

331b/332a    In the remaining three sections one should perform the first section [again], [but] ascending to the fourth, an intervening note, and the octave [respectively].

332b/333a    One should ascend to higher and higher notes in order, omitting the lower notes one by one. This is the practice in all rāgas.

It is significant that in general Śārṅgadeva does not regard the second, third and fourth sections as independent musical structures, requiring separate description, but as successive *expansions* of the material of the first section. The example of Madhyamādi quoted above is unfortunately the only case in which Śārṅgadeva describes the second, third, and fourth sections in full; however, this example clearly shows that the technique of development adopted was that which we have termed 'internal scalar expansion'. This is demonstrated in Figure 3.

Several other features of Example 6 may also be compared directly with modern rāgālāp:

(1) The note most emphasised in a particular section (e.g. g′ in section III) is not necessarily the highest note touched (cf. p. 148).

(2) When the upper tonic has been reached (section IV) notes of the upper octave may also be introduced (cf. p. 147).

(3) Strict scale-order is modified by a tendency to omit the notes 3 and 7, which is evidently a characteristic of the rāga (cf. p. 151).

(4) A tendency to omit the lower notes as higher ones are reached, observable at the beginning of sections II and III, is explicitly mentioned by Śārṅgadeva (VI. 332a–333b, translated above; cf. p. 151).

Śārṅgadeva describes the function of rāgālapti as 'demonstration' (*prakaṭīkaraṇa*) (III. 189), and states that rāgālapti must emphasise the important notes and ornamentation of the rāga concerned (III. 196). His examples in chapter VI therefore provide information about the modal structure of various thirteenth-century rāgas, and the earliest direct evidence for Indian ornamentation practice (some four centuries before Somanātha's notated ornaments); these aspects deserve further study. Since no metrical structure is prescribed, it may be assumed that rhythm and tempo were free, and the evidence for the use of internal scalar expansion suggests that performance was normally improvised, using the same basic technique that is used today. Thus in almost every respect — from its function as an improvised modal prelude to the actual form and techniques employed — rāgālapti as described in the thirteenth century resembles rāgālāp as performed in the dhrupad and instrumental traditions today.

### (c) Conclusions

We have argued that the svaraprastāra technique of note-permutation is not an important structural feature of rāgālāp. Rather, the course of melodic development at every stage is determined by 'internal scalar expansion'. Within the structure that thus evolves, more or less extensive repetition of individual notes and phrases gives scope for imaginative variation in treatment, and is used to accomplish gradual transitions or to highlight, by delay and/or repetition, important climaxes. We have seen that these techniques are used in both the instrumental and dhrupad traditions.

The brevity of Example 6 supports Sachs' contention (1944: 191) that the extreme length of some modern ālāp-performances is 'a modern development that should not be mistaken for a heritage from antiquity'. It is no doubt significant that the essential technique and form of rāgālāp can still be expressed very concisely (cf. Example 10), and that in extended performance, greater length is attained by the varied repetition of material rather than by the introduction of any additional techniques. However, Śārṇgadeva's examples were themselves no doubt considerably elaborated in performance; the extent of such elaboration can only be guessed.

Since the gradual expansion of range that characterises the whole structure of rāgālāp is already inherent in the technique of internal scalar expansion, we can view the form of rāgālāp as the direct outcome of the technique of improvisation traditionally adopted by the performer. Although it was employed in a scale-exercise (the prastāra alamkāra) by the eighth century or earlier (see p. 148), evidence for the systematic application of this technique in improvised rāga-exposition is lacking until the thirteenth century. It may be significant that the conception of a rāga as an ascending and descending scale, based on a universal ground-note or tonic, did not gain theoretical expression until the Muslim period.[10] No such conception is displayed in notated melodies (for example, the melodies of the Kudumiyāmalai Inscription — Widdess: in press) or theoretical sources of the pre-Muslim period. Śārṇgadeva's description of the technique and form of rāgālapti, in which note-by-note scalar expansion is based on a 'fixed' (*sthāyī*) tonic or ground-note, therefore marks an important stage in the development of Indian music.

---

10   In the *Svaramelakalānidhi* of Rāmāmātya (1550).

### III. The dhrupad composition

The second part of the performance, after the ālāp has been completed, is dominated by the text, melody and rhythmic structure of the dhrupad composition. This is usually in Cautāl, a tāla of twelve beats, and is performed in slow or moderate tempo. In extended performances, several compositions may be sung in sequence, in which case the first is usually in Cautāl, the second in Dhamār (fourteen beats), and the third in Sūltāl (ten beats), Pañcam Savārī (fifteen beats) or some other tāla.[11] Each composition is followed by 'divisions' before the next is taken up, and the tempo gradually increases from slow to fast.

We confine our attention to the Cautāl class of compositions, which we illustrate with two examples. Example 12 (p. 174) is a composition attributed to Haridās (a *bhakti* poet of the late sixteenth century) in four sections: sthāyi, antarā, samcārī and ābhog. The text and melody are transcribed from Bhātkhande (*KPM* II: 108ff). The basic drum pattern (*thekā*) is shown at (b) for the first measure of the sthāyi: this is to be repeated (with variations) throughout.

Example 13 (p. 177), also a composition attributed to Haridās, is in two sections only, sthāyi and antarā. The transcription is in two parts. Example 13(a) shows a simplified melodic outline without ornamentation, based on two recorded performances of the composition by the same artist, Pandit Siyārām Tiwāri.[12] The first performance was broadcast by All India Radio *c.* 1959 (I am grateful to Mr William Coates for a recording of this performance); the second was recorded by the author at Patna in 1976. Example 13(b) shows the composition as performed in the recording of *c.* 1959, showing repetition of the sthāyi and ornamentation.

The translations that precede Examples 12 and 13 have been kindly provided by Dr R.S. McGregor, who also advised on transliteration.

In view of the changes in the structure of many North Indian rāgas that are known to have occurred since the sixteenth century (Jairazbhoy 1971: 92ff), it is unlikely that the melodies of dhrupad compositions as they are sung today are more than a few generations old; similarly, the attribution of dhrupad texts to fifteenth- and sixteenth-century authors cannot, in most cases, be proven. However, there is evidence that dhrupad compositions preserve a musical form first attested in the thirteenth century. The principal features of this form are that it is cyclic, both rhythmically and formally; and that the antarā and ābhog emphasise a higher register than the sthāyi and samcārī.

#### (a) Tāla

The twelve beats of Cautāl are counted in four groups: 4 + 4 + 2 + 2. The first beat of each group may be indicated by the singer with a clap (*tālī*) (hence Cautāl, 'four(-clap) tāla'). Thus

11  Śrī N.C. Bural has drawn my attention to a further class of dhrupad composition in which the four sections employ different tālas.

12  The melodic outline is derived not primarily from the slow-tempo renderings with which each performance begins (see Example 13b), but from the double-speed (*dūgun*) variations subsequently performed (not shown in Example 13); in these double-speed versions there is less ornamentation, and there are fewer melodic differences between the two performances.

claps, marked X 2 3 4 in Example 7 below, occur on beats 1, 5, 9 and 11. Beats 3 and 7 are indicated with a silent wave of the hand (*khāli*), marked 0 in Example 7. The first beat of the cycle is the most emphasised, and performs an important structural rôle; it is termed *sam* (from Sanskrit *samnipāta*, a clap of the hands) and is marked X in Example 7. The twelve-beat pattern is repeated cyclically as many times as necessary for the completion of the composition and the variations that follow. In this procedure the sam serves both as the completion of one cycle and as the beginning of the next. This can be seen from the basic drum pattern (thekā), shown in Example 7; this underlines the two groups of four at the beginning of the cycle, but towards the end includes idiomatic off-beat accents that resolve on the first beat of the next cycle.

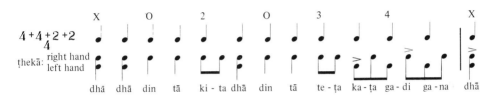

Example 7

The thekā serves merely as the starting-point for complex rhythmic variations on the part of the drum-player; these, like the singer's variations, must always end on the first beat of a tāla-cycle.

### (b) Melodic structure

The full-length dhrupad text comprises four lines of a variable number of syllables, with end-rhyme of one or more syllables. The text-lines correspond to the four musical sections sthāyi, antarā, samcāri and ābhog (see Example 12). The verbal rhyme may be accompanied by musical rhyme: compare Example 12, bars 4, 8 and 16, and Example 13(a), bars 4–5 and 9–10. Individual sections or particular bars may be repeated at the discretion of the performer, before proceeding to the next: thus in Example 13(b), the sthāyi is repeated several times before the antarā is taken up.

In performance an important rôle is played by the mukhrā, a phrase derived from the sthāyi of the composition (and thus distinct from the mukhrā of ālāp (see p. 146), to which it is, however, similar in function). This phrase is repeated to bring the complete performance of the song to an end. Thus the melody, like the rhythmic pattern, is cyclic, in that it returns to its own starting-point.

The mukhrā may also be repeated after both sthāyi and antarā, but not usually between samcāri and ābhog, which are normally sung consecutively without a break.

In Examples 12 and 13 the mukhṛā are as follows:

Example 8

In each case, the mukhṛā comprises the first sam or emphasised beat of the sthāyī, preceded by an anacrusis of several beats. It may be followed by part or the whole of the remainder of the sthāyī, except at the conclusion of the performance, which must end on the sam of the mukhṛā (marked [⌢]).

In Example 12, the mukhṛā (comprising the grammatically isolated exclamation 'O Lady!') occurs at the conclusion of sthāyī, antarā and ābhog, and would be followed in performance by repetition of part or all of the sthāyī.[13] In Example 13, the mukhṛā is repeated after sthāyī and antarā. Both the performances on which Example 13 is based concluded with a *tihāī* – a thrice-repeated variation of the mukhṛā – followed by an extempore descending phrase in free tempo ending on the tonic (see Example 9).

It is often stated that the melody of the sthāyī moves in the lower tetrachord of the middle octave and in the lower octave, while that of the antarā rises to the upper tetrachord of the middle octave and enters the upper octave (cf. Kaufmann 1968: 25f). However, it has been pointed out by Wade (1971: 196) and van der Meer (1977: 46 and n. 23) that neither in khyāl nor in dhrupad compositions is this structure necessarily followed in the sthāyī. In both the examples under consideration (Examples 12 and 13) the melody of the sthāyī covers the *whole*

Example 9

---

13  Since this exclamation occurs after the rhyme, it may be regarded as an anacrusis to line 1, rather than as the conclusion to lines 1, 2 and 4.

of the middle octave and enters the upper octave.[14] In these examples the distinguishing features of the antarā are:

(1) a characteristic opening formula: a rising phrase leading to the upper tonic, which is then repeated in the manner of a reciting-note;

(2) development of the upper tetrachord of the middle octave and lower tetrachord of the upper octave, including

(3) a phrase that rises to a higher note than was reached in the sthāyī.

Thus in Examples 12 and 13 the antarā melody moves predominantly in the upper part of the middle octave and in the upper octave, and stresses the upper tonic. Both examples begin with the 'antarā-formula', rising from the fourth or fifth to the upper tonic, which is then repeated. The climax of the whole song comes in the second (Example 12) or third (Example 13) bar of the antarā, where the melody ascends one or two notes higher than the highest note of the sthāyī. In general, these features of the antarā would appear to be true of most dhrupad and khyāl compositions.[15]

The relationship between the sthāyī and antarā on the one hand, and the saṃcārī and ābhog (where present) on the other, is the subject of some disagreement. According to the dhrupad compositions with musical notation, collected and published by Bhātkhaṇḍe (*KPM*) and Rājā Nawāb Ālī (*MN*), the saṃcārī normally moves in a similar register to the sthāyī, with which it may share melodic material, but frequently emphasises the fifth; the ābhog closely resembles the antarā (see Example 12). The overall form is therefore A B A'+B.

It will be recalled that the saṃcārī and ābhog are performed consecutively, without any intervening repetition of the mukhṛā (p. 161). Evidence presented by Śrīvastava (1977: 30f. and footnotes 41 and 44) suggests that until comparatively recent times the saṃcārī–ābhog was regarded as a single section, called simply *ābhog* (according to Śrīvastava the term *saṃcārī* does not appear in this context before the nineteenth century). This merely implies a difference of terminology, however, not of musical structure.

According to several modern accounts of dhrupad, for example that of Kaufmann (1968: 25f), the combined saṃcārī–ābhog is misleadingly termed *saṃcārī*. The term *ābhog* is then applied to a repetition of the mukhṛā or sthāyī at the conclusion of the song. This terminology is open to question, because the so-called ābhog is not a distinct section either in text or melody, but merely a repetition of the mukhṛā (which is repeated elsewhere) or sthāyī.

Differing conceptions of the structure of the dhrupad composition are set out below, as they would be applied to a composition in sixteen bars (cf. Example 12): (1) the original division into three sections, called *udgrāha* (= sthāyī), antarā and ābhoga; (2) the division of Bhātkhaṇḍe and others into four sections, sthāyī, antarā, saṃcārī and ābhog; (3) the interpretation of Kaufmann and others.

14  A statistical analysis of the 222 dhrupad melodies in *MN* reveals that in 104 cases (47 per cent) the sthāyī melody ascends to the upper tonic or beyond. The highest note reached in any sthāyī melody is 4 (no. 79).

15  In *MN*, the antarā extends to a higher note than is reached in the sthāyī in all except 26 cases (12 per cent). There are only six melodies in which the antarā does not ascend to the upper tonic (nos. 30, 88, 124, 149, 190, and 232 (*sic*)).

Hypothetical
dhrupad
composition:    bars

| | | 1 | 2 | 3 | 4 | 5 | 6 | 7 | 8 | 9 | 10 | 11 | 12 | 13 | 14 | 15 | 16 | ‖ | 1 | 2 | 3 | 4 |
|---|---|---|---|---|---|---|---|---|---|---|---|---|---|---|---|---|---|---|---|---|---|---|
| (1) | | udgrāha | | | | antarā | | | | ābhoga | | | | | | | | ‖ | (udgrāha) | | | |
| (2) | | sthāyī | | | | antarā | | | | samcārī | | | | ābhog | | | | ‖ | (sthāyi) | | | |
| (3) | | sthāyī | | | | antarā | | | | samcārī | | | | | | | | ‖ | ābhog | | | |

For the purpose of the historical investigations that follow, interpretation (3) is rejected.

### (c) 'Dhrupad/kīrtana form' and *dhruva prabandha*

The melodic structure of the typical dhrupad composition, outlined above, is not confined to
the dhrupad genre. Khyāl compositions, like many dhrupad compositions, have sthāyi and antarā
only; but the South Indian kīrtana (a classical devotional song) resembles the four-part dhrupad
(see p. 145). Example 14 (after Kaufmann 1976: 220f)[16] shows a kīrtana melody in three principal sections. The pallavī (bars 1–2), equivalent to the sthāyī of dhrupad, emphasises the lower
tonic and middle octave (other examples ascend to the upper tonic, as do many sthāyī melodies).
The anupallavī (= antarā) (bars 2–4) emphasises the upper tonic, and moves in a generally high
register; note the opening 'antarā-formula' (p. 163). The third section, caranam, is equivalent in
length to the pallavī and anupallavī together. Bars 4–5 move in a similar register to the pallavī
but emphasise the fifth (cf. Example 12, bars 9–10), whereas bars 6–8 repeat the material of
the anupallavī. The caranam is therefore equivalent to the samcārī–ābhog of dhrupad. The
whole caranam may be omitted in shorter examples (this is often the case with kriti compositions – kīrtanas in which the musical element is more important than the religious), which
therefore resemble short dhrupads or khyāls. In Example 14, the whole of the pallavī is repeated
as a refrain after pallavī, anupallavī and caranam.[17]

We can therefore recognise a 'dhrupad/kīrtana form', in either four sections (A B A'+B) or
two (A B), plus refrain, that is common to both northern and southern traditions of Indian art-
music. While the remote origins of the form are unknown, it is probable that the mediaeval
Hindu devotional (*bhakti*) movements, which originated in South India in the later first
millennium A.D. and spread to the North by the fifteenth century, were responsible for its
wide distribution and lasting popularity, for the texts of many if not most dhrupads, khyāls,
kīrtanas and kritis are devotional in content, and are in many cases ascribed to bhakti saints
(e.g. Haridās). The bhakti poets adopted popular rather than literary verse-forms for their songs
(padas), and it may therefore be in folk-music, rather than in the forms of art-music described
by Bharata, Dattila and other early writers, that the antecedents of dhrupad/kīrtana form are to
be found.

The first evidence for dhrupad/kīrtana form in classical literature is probably the thirteenth-
century description by Śārṅgadeva (*SSR* IV: 315ff) of a type of vocal composition (*prabandha*)

16  This example is reproduced by kind permission of Indiana University Press.
17  According to Kaufmann, the song ends 'with *MA* (F)', presumably on beat 1, bar 2 (marked
[⌒] in Example 14).

called *dhruva-prabandha*. This was the first of seven types of composition, all apparently sharing a similar structure, collectively called *sālaga-sūḍa prabandhas*. This category of compositions is first mentioned here and in the *Saṅgītasamayāsāra* of Pārśvadeva[18] (twelfth or thirteenth century).

Śārṅgadeva's account runs as follows:

315   Where there is an udgrāha, it should be in two [sub] sections (*khaṇḍa*) with one melody (*ekadhātu*). After this there should be a section [in a] somewhat high [register]. These three sections should be executed twice.

316   Then there should be an ābhoga of two sections, of which the first section is in two [sub] sections with one melody, and the second section [in a] higher [register].

317   In some cases, the name of the person to be praised is included in this high section. [There is] a cadence in the first [sub] section of the udgrāha. This is the *dhruvaka* [i.e. dhruva-prabandha].

It is clear from this brief account that the dhruva-prabandha had three principal sections. The first, called *udgrāha*, was itself divided into two subsections, identical or similar as to melody (*dhātu*). The second section is not named by Śārṅgadeva, but the name *antarā* is supplied by the fourteenth-century commentator Siṃhabhūpāla. The 'high' register of this section invites comparison with the antarā/anupallavi of modern dhrupad/kīrtana form.

The third section, *ābhoga*, was divisible into two sections. These repeated the characteristics of the udgrāha ('two [sub] sections with a single melody') and antarā ('higher' register) respectively. Therefore, the structure of the dhruva-prabandha was A B A+B; and we can therefore equate the udgrāha with the modern sthāyī/pallavi, the antarā with the modern antarā/anupallavi, and the ābhoga with the saṃcārī—ābhog/caraṇam of dhrupad/kīrtana form.

The dhruva-prahandha ended (v. 317) with a repetition of the first subsection of the udgrāha, that is, the first line or phrase of the song. This leads us to the important conclusion that the form, like dhrupad/kīrtana form, was cyclic: that is, the melody returned to its own starting-point.

Śārṅgadeva's account presents four difficulties;

(1) no reference is made to the repetition of a refrain after the first and second sections, as frequently found in dhrupad/kīrtana form (see above, p. 161);

(2) although the form is called dhruva-prabandha, the term *dhruva* is not applied to any of its sections, or otherwise explained;

(3) it is stated that the udgrāha and antarā are both to be repeated before proceeding to the ābhoga (v. 315); this procedure is not usual in dhrupad/kīrtana form;

---

18   The evidence of this and other sources is discussed in the Appendix, below. The relationship between dhrupad and dhruva-prabandha has been briefly examined by Prajñānānanda (1965: 172ff), te Nijenhuis (1974: 82ff), and Śrīvastava (1977: 22ff).

(4) the division of the first section into two subsections with the same melody is not a recognised feature of dhrupad/kirtana form.

Points (1) and (3) (dealt with further below) may perhaps indicate either differences between thirteenth-century performance-practice and that of today, or inaccuracies in Śārṅgadeva's very brief account. Evidence for a refrain, however, can be found in vv. 332–3 of the same source, which describes a closely related genre called *mantha-prabandha* (also of the sālaga-sūda category). Here a section called (significantly) *dhruva* is said to be repeated after udgrāha, antarā and ābhog.[19] The term *dhruva* may therefore have already acquired its later meaning of 'refrain', and the omission of the term in vv. 315–17 may be connected with the omission there (perhaps accidental) of any reference to a refrain (except at the conclusion of the song). The structure of the mantha-prabandha was shared by the five further varieties of sālaga-sūda prabandha (v. 335). In these circumstances, it seems likely that the dhruva-prabandha also had a refrain, and that this was called *dhruva*.[20]

The structure of the dhruva-prabandha is reconstructed below, and placed in parallel with that of the modern dhrupad and kirtana; inferences from and additions to the information supplied by Śārṅgadeva are indicated by square brackets.

| melodic structure | dhruva-prabandha | | dhrupad | kīrtana |
|---|---|---|---|---|
| A $(= a_1 + a_2)$ | udgrāha | A | sthāyī | pallavī |
| $[a_1?]$ | [dhruva?] | $a_1$ | mukhṛā | pallavī |
| B* | [antarā] | B* | antarā | anupallavī |
| $[a_1?]$ | [dhruva?] (repeat the above) | $a_1$ | mukhṛā | pallavī |
| A $(= a_1 + a_2)$ <br> B* | } ābhoga | A'<br>B* | samcārī<br>ābhog | } caraṇam |
| $a_1$ | [dhruva] | $a_1$ | mukhṛā | pallavī |

\* = high register

The only difficulties that remain are (3) and (4). A simple explanation of (3) would be that the repetition of udgrāha and antarā, mentioned by Śārṅgadeva (v. 315), refers merely to the repetition of the *melodies* of these sections in the ābhoga that follows. As for (4), although no detailed study of the formal types of Indian melody is yet available, one can find a number of melodies in published collections that have sthāyī in the form a + a or a + a', where the second half is a repetition or variation of the first. In most cases the antarā is through-composed. These

---

19  In this case the antarā is said to be optional, however.
20  This hypothesis is supported (a) by the consideration that if the udgrāha, antarā and ābhoga were not in some way separated in performance, it would be illogical to regard the udgrāha and antarā (on the one hand) as separate sections and the ābhoga (on the other hand) as a single section; and (b) by the evidence of the *Saṅgītadāmodara* (see Appendix).

examples do not occur exclusively, or indeed frequently, in the dhrupad, khyāl, kīrtana and kriti categories, since many modern art-melodies have three rather than two phrases in the sthāyī (cf. Wade 1971: 230). However, the sthāyī of Example 13 in this study exhibits the form a + a′; about twenty further examples are to be found in the collection of 222 dhrupad melodies in *MN*; and thirty-four more in Fox Strangways' selection of fifty-nine didactic songs from Poona (1914: 301–16). Śārṅgadeva was evidently describing a melody-type that still exists, though other types are equally or more important in the current classical repertory.

In conclusion, the dhruva-prabandha was a cyclic song-form with the structure A B A+B, where B was in a high register; the first phrase of A served as a refrain (called *dhruva*?), repeated at the end of the song and also, perhaps, at the ends of the first and second sections. In all these respects, the dhruva-prabandha resembles the modern dhrupad/kīrtana form, which is also found in an abbreviated form in khyāl and kriti. A similar structure appears to have been typical of all the sālaga-sūda prabandhas, a category first attested in the twelfth or thirteenth century. Śārṅgadeva's account of dhruva-prabandha, like that of rāgālapti, illustrates the remarkable continuity of a musical form over a period of six hundred years, a period during which many changes in North Indian music (especially in the structure of individual rāgas) are known to have taken place.

## IV. Nom tom and bāṃt

It has not been possible to give detailed consideration to the nom tom and bāṃt sections of a dhrupad performance — sections that are often given the most prominence by performers. The following brief observations are offered, however, as a basis for further investigation.

(1) The formal structures of nom tom and bāṃt are derived, in essence, from those of the preceding rāgālāp and dhrupad composition respectively. Thus the melodic outline of nom tom usually echoes the rising and falling 'arches' of the rāgālāp, although less attention may be given to the development of individual notes. The lay-bāṃt variations are directly derived (by a process of strict diminution) from the composition itself; in the bol-bāṃt variations the text and melody of the composition are more freely treated. The individuality of nom tom and bāṃt therefore rests on style and vocal technique, rather than on form.

(2) Both nom tom and bāṃt have counterparts in South Indian performance-practice (see p. 00). The nom tom style, which is derived from the *jor* and *jhālā* styles of plucked string instruments, and uses meaningless 'nom tom' syllables (perhaps derived from instrumental mnemonic syllables), is analogous to the South Indian *tānam*, a style derived from the idiom of the vīṇā, which features prominently in the performance of *rāgam-tānam-pallavī* and in instrumental (rarely vocal) kriti. The strict diminution of lay-bāṃt has its counterpart in South Indian *anuloma* which may also involve augmentation (cf. Widdess 1977). The South Indian *niraval* technique, in which the melody is varied while the rhythm and words of the song remain intact, perhaps bears some resemblance to the bol-bāṃt of dhrupad. However, the relationship of South Indian and North Indian improvisation-techniques requires detailed investigation.

These parallels suggest that nom tom and bāṃṭ represent universal and ancient features of Indian performance-practice. This is confirmed by the earliest Sanskrit musicological text, the *Nāṭyaśāstra* (early centuries A.D.), which refers to the use of instrumental mnemonics in the prelude (*upohana* or *bahirgīta*) to songs (XXXI: 323), and to diminution (*nivṛtti*) in the *aparāntaka* song (XXXI: 248).

## V. Conclusions

In summary, we offer the following conclusions regarding the form and history of North Indian ālāp and dhrupad.

(1) The form of the rāgālāp derives from a technique of improvisation, namely, the development of material through internal scalar expansion. Permutation of notes in the manner of svaraprastāra is not exhibited in the examples studied.

(2) The form of rāgālāp is first described by Śārṅgadeva in the thirteenth century. Examples provided by this authority are shorter than modern examples, but identical in technique and form.

(3) The structure of the four-part dhrupad composition may be expressed as A B A′+B. This form is obscured in some accounts by different usages of terminology.

(4) This form is also found in the South Indian kīrtana, and like that of rāgālāp, is described in the thirteenth century by Śārṅgadeva. Its wide dissemination and lasting popularity may be due to its adoption (perhaps from folk-music) by the bhakti movement.

There is therefore strong evidence that the performance of ālāp and dhrupad in North India today preserves musical forms that have been current in the Indian tradition for at least six hundred years.

Examples 10–13 use the following special symbols:

Example 10. Rāg Bhairav

Example 11. Rāg Bāgeśrī

* Initial sounding of tonic by the singer, during tuning of instruments, omitted in the recording.
† Interlude by sitar accompanist omitted in the transcription.

170

Duration (with interludes) 13½ min.

Example 12. Rāg Alhaiyā Bilāval

Text:

| | |
|---|---|
| 1 (sthāyī) | Āja aura kāla aura dina prati aura aura dekhie rasika girirāja **dharana**. *Māi rī!* . . . |
| 2 (antarā) | Dina prati nai chabi barane so kauna? Kaba pāna kīje? Rijha rahie sadā hi **sarana**. *Māi rī!* . . . |
| 3 (saṃcārī) | Sābhā syāma aṃga aṃga lājata koṭika anaṃga chavi ki uṭhata taraṃga viśva ko mana**harani**. |
| 4 (ābhog) | Catrabhūja prabhū giridhāri ko sarūpa sundara dekhie siṃgāra bāga varana **barana**. *Māi rī!* . . . |

**Bold** = rhyme
*italics* = mukhṛā

Translation:

1  O Lady! Look today, tomorrow and every day at the
   attire of the elegant King of the Mountain.*
2  O Lady! Who can describe his beauty which changes day by day? When shall we taste it?
   May he who is our refuge always be pleased with us.
3  Śyām's* limbs are so beautiful as to put a myriad Kāmdevs to shame.
   Their incomparable beauty captivates the heart of the universe.
4  O Lady! Behold the beautiful form of the four-armed Lord who held up the mountain.*
   His array and the colour of his robe are splendid.

*Kṛṣṇa

Example 13a. Rāg Asāvarī

Text:

1 (sthāyī)    *Bāra bāra naina* kāma lāla lāla daura kāra
              kāra bhamarā nike maṇḍarāta **haiṃ**.

2 (antarā)    Atara sacātura bhāeṃ haiṃ triyā ke basa
              jāka dṛga dekhe mīna khanjana **lajāta haiṃ**.

Translation:

1  Time and time again our eyes, flushed with love, are drawn [to Kṛṣṇa], like bees
   gathering honey which fly delightfully [around a flower].

2  All perfumes acknowledge the superiority of the lady* the sight of whose eyes puts the
   fish and wagtails to shame.

   *Rādhā

Example 13b

Example 14. Mārgahindoḷa rāga (Ādi-tāla)

## Appendix: Additional evidence for the form of dhruva-prabandha

Besides *SSR*, the following sources give brief accounts of dhruva-prabandha:

(A) Pārśvadeva: *Saṅgitasamayāsāra* (eleventh or twelfth century: cited in Prajñānānanda 1965: 191).

(B) Ṣudhakalāsa: *Saṅgitopanisatsāroddhāra* (A.D. 1350; ed. U.P. Shah, Baroda 1961; I. 54).

(C) Śubhaṅkara: *Saṅgitadāmodara* (sixteenth century; ed. G. Śāstri and G. Mukhopadhyāya, Calcutta Sanskrit College Research Series, no. 11, Calcutta 1960; p. 19).

(D) Raghunātha: *Saṅgitasudhā* (A.D. 1614; cited in Prajñānānanda 1965: 192f)

(E) Veṅkatamakhī: *Caturdaṇḍiprakāśikā* (A.D. 1620; cited in Prajñānānanda 1965: 193).

(D) and (E) are clearly derived from *SSR*, to which they add little information. They are the only sources beside *SSR* to mention the distinction in range between udgrāha and antarā. (A), (B), and (C) may therefore represent a different tradition or traditions: the dhruva-prabandha is described in different terms in each of them.

The sources (A), (B) and (C) all divide the dhruva-prabandha into three principal sections. In (A) the first of these is termed udgrāha, and is said to comprise two subsections (cf. *SSR*). The second, termed *aṅghrī*, is described as 'equal to the udgrāha (*tattulya*) [in length?]'. The third section, not named, comprises repetition of the udgrāha and aṅghrī, which latter follows without a break (*sakṛd api*).

According to (B), the three sections are called *udgrāha*, *dhruva*, and *ābhoga* respectively, and are each divided into two subsections (*pada*). A possible explanation for this description, which is not supplemented by any further musical information and which appears to conflict with both *SSR* and (A), is provided by (C). This source first repeats the description of (B), dividing the three principal sections into two subsections (*khaṇḍa*) each. The six *khaṇḍas* are then named as follows: *udgrāha*, *dhruva*, *antarā*, *dhruva*, *ābhoga*, *dhruva*. This account suggests the following relationship between the descriptions of *SSR*, (A), (B) and (C):

| SSR | (A) | | (B) | | (C) |
|---|---|---|---|---|---|
| udgrāha | udgrāha | } | udgrāha | { | udgrāha |
| [dhruva] | | | | | dhruva |
| [antarā] | aṅghrī | } | dhruva | { | antarā |
| [dhruva] | | | | | dhruva |
| ābhoga | ? | } | ābhoga | { | ābhoga |
| [dhruva] | | | | | dhruva |

The testimony of (C) supports the hypothesis that a refrain called *dhruva* was sung after udgrāha, antarā and ābhoga (see p. 166). The four sources also suggest that the usage of terminology regarding musical forms varied in the twelfth to sixteenth centuries, as it does today.

Bibliography

Bhātkhande, V.N. 1954–9. *Kramik pustak mālikā*, 6 vols., Hathras
Fox Strangways, A.H. 1914. *The music of Hindostan*, Oxford
Jairazbhoy, N.A. 1961. 'Svaraprastāra in North Indian music', *Bulletin of the School of Oriental and African Studies* XXIV
Jairazbhoy, N.A. 1971. *The rāgs of North Indian music*, London
Kaufmann, W. 1968. *The rāgas of North India*, Bloomington Oriental Series 1, Bloomington, Indiana
Kaufmann, W. 1976. *The rāgas of South India*, Bloomington, Indiana
Mataṅga, *Bṛhaddesī*, ed. K. Sambāsiva Sāstrī, Trivandrum, 1928
Nawāb Āli Khān, Rājā 1952. *Māriphunnagmāt (Ma'ārif al-nagmāt*, Hindi edn), Hathras
Prajñānānanda, Swāmi 1965. *A historical study of Indian music*, Calcutta
Sachs, C. 1944. *The rise of music in the ancient world, East and West*, London
Sārmā, P. (ed.) 1972. *Sahasras*, Sangīt Naṭak Academy, Delhi
Sārṅgadeva, *Saṅgītaratnākara*, ed. S. Subrahmaṇya Sāstrī, Adyar Library, Madras, vol. II 1959; vol. III 1951
Srīvastava, I. 1977. 'Dhrupada, a study of its origin, historical development, structure and present state', unpublished doctoral thesis, Utrecht
te Nijenhuis, E. 1974. *Indian music: history and structure*, Leiden
van der Meer, W. 1977. 'Hindustani music in the twentieth century', unpublished doctoral thesis, Utrecht
Wade, B.D. 1971. *Khyāl: a study in Hindustani classical vocal music*, 2 vols., University Microfilms, Ann Arbor, Michigan
Widdess, D.R. 1977. '*Trikāla*: a demonstration of augmentation and diminution from South India', *Musica Asiatica* I, Oxford
Widdess, D.R., in press. 'The Kudumiyāmalai Inscription: a source of early Indian music in notation', *Musica Asiatica* II, Oxford

# Theme and variation in kora music: a preliminary study of 'Tutu Jara' as performed by Amadu Bansang Jobate

LUCY DURÁN

Amadu Bansang Jobate, a Mandinka professional musician from The Gambia, is one of the leading exponents of the kora, the twenty-one-string harp—lute that is unique to West Africa (Plate 1). His style of playing combines the characteristic idiom of his native region, the Gambian upper-river area, with a highly individual mode of expression. Amadu Bansang is known especially for his instrumental solos, such as that on a recording currently used by Radio Gambia as their signature tune,[1] but he is also a skilled accompanist, since for many years he worked regularly with the eminent singer Bamba Suso, now deceased. Although he has an extensive repertoire of about two hundred pieces, there are a few items which he considers his specialities. Of these, 'Tutu Jara' is one of the most important tunes in the traditional upper-river repertoire, and Amadu Bansang's interpretation of this piece is unusually varied. The following study arises from a six-month study period with him, first in The Gambia and later in England.[2]

## I. The kora: area of distribution, repertoire, tuning and playing technique[3]

The kora is played exclusively by male musicians (Mandinka *Jali*) from the professional musicians' class of the Manding peoples, who are found in Mali (part of which is postulated as the original Manding homeland), Guinea, Guinea-Bissau, Senegal, The Gambia and the north-west Ivory

1 'Jula Faso'; it may be heard on Radio Gambia at 12 midday and 5 p.m. daily.
2 The assistance given by the British Institute of Recorded Sound towards field research in The Gambia is gratefully acknowledged; I am also grateful to Dr Anthony King for introducing me to Amadu Bansang. Amadu's visit to England (his first trip outside West Africa) was sponsored by the Ethnomusicological Audio Visual Archive of Cambridge University. Numerous recordings of his 'Tutu Jara' are deposited at both the BIRS and EAVA archives.
3 More detailed discussion of the kora's construction and tuning may be found in King 1972, and of the repertoire and social context of the music and musicians, in Knight 1973, chapters I—III.

Plate 1. The Mandinka kora, played by Amadu Bansang Jobate (courtesy of the Ethnomusicological Audio Visual Archive, Cambridge)

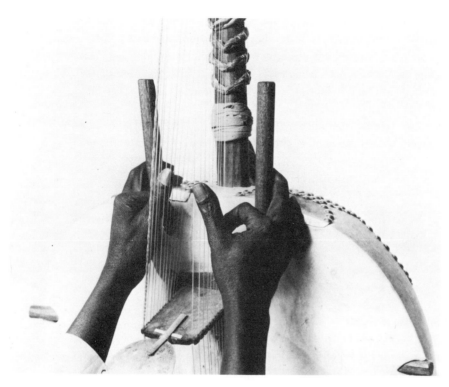

Plate 2. The kora: close-up of the player's hands (courtesy of the Ethnomusicological Audio Visual Archive, Cambridge)

Coast. It is said by the musicians to have originated in the Kaabu region of Guinea-Bissau and is in its present form at least two hundred years old;[4] part of its repertoire is borrowed from the two older melody instruments of the Jali, the balo (eighteen-key xylophone) and the kontingo (small five-string lute). The kora is used mainly to accompany song; though instrumental solos and duets are not uncommon, they are always based on the song accompaniments. Most of the songs commemorate the great Manding heroes and patrons of the Jali. The two main regional styles of the Gambian kora, the upper-river or Tilibo (eastern) and the Casamance (southern Senegal) style, are differentiated by repertoire, instrumental technique, tuning, vocal style and language.

The unique feature of the kora is its division of the twenty-one strings into two parallel planes at right angles to the sound table, lying on either side of a raised notched bridge, with eleven strings on the left and ten on the right. The kora is plucked with the thumbs and index fingers of both hands (Plate 2). Of the four heptatonic tunings used on the kora, only the one

4 The earliest known reference to the kora is by Mungo Park (1799: 278), who describes it as the 'korri', 'a large harp with eighteen strings'.

known as *sauta* will be given here since it is the tuning commonly used for 'Tutu Jara'. Sauta may be compared to a just-intonation scale, with a sharp fourth and a very slightly sharp third and seventh.[5] Amadu Bansang shows a general preference for this tuning, and certainly the sharp fourth (the only note which distinguishes the sauta from the *hardino* tuning) figures prominently in his 'Tutu Jara';[6] some other players, however, appear to play 'Tutu Jara' in the hardino tuning.[7]

As on some other African instruments, the notes of the scale are distributed between the right and left hands, so that consecutive pitches are obtained by plucking alternately with

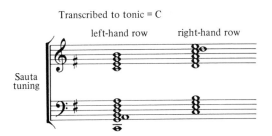

Example 1. Distribution of pitches

either hand (see Example 1).[8] This has a considerable influence on musical patterns, which is especially evident in pieces originally composed on the kora, but is also present in adaptations for the kora from the repertoire of other instruments, as in the case of 'Tutu Jara', originally a kontingo piece.

## II. The structure of kora music: kumbengo and birimintingo[9]

Kora players divide the instrumental aspect of performance into two components, the *kumbengo* (a recurrent theme) and the *birimintingo* (variation and embellishment). The term 'kumbengo'[10]

5   For intervallic measurement in cents see King 1972.
6   In contrast with Knight's statement (1973: 310) that 'the kumbengo does not include pitch four'.
7   E.g. the transcription of 'Tutu Jara', in Knight, 1973, vol. 2, p. 1.
8   The two-stave notation used here is in accordance with the transcription method used by King (1972 and 1974), in which the lowest pitch is transcribed as C. (An alternative method is used by Knight, 1971.) Actual pitch on Amadu Bansang's kora varies between C and F. The bar lines are for convenience of reading and do not indicate stress. The only special symbols required for purposes of this study are an X (indicating the rhythmic tap; see section II) and a circle around the notes which are damped (see section III).
9   For a discussion of the two vocal components of kora music, *donkilo* (choral refrain) and *sataro* (improvised solo recitation), see Knight 1973: ch. VIII–IX, and King 1974.
10   From *kungo* ('head') and *bengo* ('meeting').

(plural *kumbengolu*) is used in several contexts,[11] all of which are related to its general meaning of strings which, when sounded together, are in agreement. This accord of certain strings refers primarily to octaves and fifths. The origin of the word 'birimintingo' is obscure, though it may possibly be onomatopoeic for the rapid descending ornamental phrases that are idiomatic to the kora.[12]

The recurrent theme consists of a short, usually bipartite phrase, whose second half is almost always a modification of the first. The theme usually corresponds in length to a rhythmic pattern (*konkondiro*) which may be tapped on the gourd resonator of the kora by another musician, and which provides the rhythmic framework for extended variations. The balance between kumbengo and birimintingo depends mostly on the circumstances of the performance (for example, birimintingo takes on greater importance in instrumental solos), but also on the skill and attitude of the performer, and on the piece itself. Some items, such as 'Tutu Jara', are apparently more suitable for ornamentation than others.

Previous writings on the kora may have given the impression that for each piece there is only one form of kumbengo common to all players.[13] Apart from differences in individual style and interpretation,[14] pieces may vary considerably on a regional basis. Some have more than just one kumbengo, and these may be performed as separate items or, in some cases, as a continuous set of related items. There has also been a tendency to regard the kumbengo as the 'fixed' part of a kora piece,[15] and the birimintingo as the improvised element; however, this is not strictly true in the case of 'Tutu Jara' and other pieces as played by Amadu Bansang.

### III. 'Tutu Jara' and its rôle in Amadu Bansang's repertoire

'Tutu Jara' is considered one of the oldest and most prestigious pieces in the Tilibo repertoire. It may be used to accompany any improvised text[16] in praise of the musician's patron, or some other important person. Its own text, from which the title is derived, concerns a princess who, as her children were always stillborn, prayed for help to a snake (*tutu*). When her next child lived, she named him after the snake to show her gratitude, *Jara* being the child's second name.

11  Kumbengo also refers to all kora strings in the relationship of an octave or a fifth to the lowest string, that is (in the notation used here) to all Cs and Gs. These are the strings which are played to check if the kora is in tune, and thus by extension the word may also be used to mean tuning. In addition, the left-hand upper C (the fourth left-hand string counting towards the player) is specifically called kumbengo since it must be present in every statement of the theme (Amadu Bansang).
12  Another etymology is suggested by Knight (1973: 69).
13  This impression may be given by the use of a single example of one kumbengo to illustrate a particular piece, as in Knight 1973 and King 1974.
14  See Durán (1978(a) for a comparison of different performers' interpretations of the same piece, 'Kelefa Saane'.
15  For example, Knight (1973: 68) describes kumbengo as a 'fixed ostinato'.
16  For melodic analysis of the vocal refrain associated with 'Tutu Jara', see Knight 1973: 312f.

'Tutu Jara' was originally a kontingo piece, though it has today become a standard part of the kora repertoire.

There are at least three reasons why 'Tutu Jara' occupies a special rôle in Amadu Bansang's repertoire: (i) because of its traditional importance, since Amadu Bansang is himself a strong traditionalist; (ii) because it was first taught to him by his father, who was a kontingo player (see the biographical note below); and (iii) because it is the favourite tune of his patron, the present Chief of Brikama. This is the tune which the chief requests whenever engaging in political discussion, since, by his own admission, it helps him to express his thoughts. As a result, 'Tutu Jara' is probably the tune which Amadu Bansang has played most often in recent years. It is not surprising, therefore, that in his performance it creates a greater impression of complexity and continual variation than any other item in his repertoire.[17]

Amadu Bansang bases his 'Tutu Jara' on four kumbengolu, shown — in the form in which he teaches them — as item (i) in Examples 5—9 (pp. 192—5). Two of these he describes as being of regional origin (Examples 5 and 9 are from Tilibo and Mali respectively), the third (Example 7) as being the 'oldest' way of playing 'Tutu Jara', and the fourth (Example 8) as his own invention. A fifth kumbengo, called 'Segu Tutu' after the Segu region in Mali from which it is said to originate, is not considered here, as Amadu Bansang treats it as a separate piece. When accompanying song, each of the four kumbengolu is usually expounded in turn, but in instrumental solos Amadu may switch rapidly back and forth from one to the other.

The four kumbengolu differ in all but a few basic features. An important unifying factor in performance, however, is the rhythmic pattern (konkondiro)[18] of four evenly spaced pulses, the first three tapped and the last silent. One of the features the four kumbengolu share is the frequent alternation between duple and triple metres. This is a feature that also occurs briefly in other pieces, but in 'Tutu Jara' it is sustained and may be regarded as an important variation

Example 2. Table of compound and simple divisions of the rhythmic pattern (konkondiro) established by the tap

---

17   A performance may be heard on 'Amadu Bansang Jobarteh: master of the kora', issued on Eavadisc record EDM 101 (Cambridge, 1979), side 1 band 3.
18   See note 8.

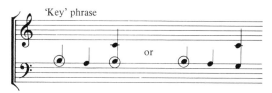

Example 3. 'Key' phrase

device. In spite of this metric alternation, the tap nevertheless remains constant (see Example 2). The main feature the kumbengolu have in common, however, is the melodic phrase shown in Example 3; this will be called the 'key' phrase, since according to Amadu Bansang it identifies 'Tutu Jara' and acts as the point in the kumbengo to which all variation must return.

A third characteristic of 'Tutu Jara', already evident in the 'key' phrase, is the extensive use of a technique known as *detero*, whereby certain strings are damped immediately after plucking,[19] either with the tip of the finger from one side of the string or with the nail from the other. In Amadu Bansang's style of playing, detero is applied to all rapid ornamental passages as well as to particular notes in the kumbengo, which in 'Tutu Jara' are the seventh, sharp fourth, and occasionally the third and sixth degrees of the scale.

Most Gambian kora players seem to base their version of 'Tutu Jara' on the Tilibo kumbengo,[20] which occurs in both simple triple and compound duple metres (Examples 5 and 6 respectively). More rarely heard in The Gambia is the 'oldest' version of 'Tutu Jara'[21] (Example 7), which is played in triple time only. Its melodic skeleton,[22] revolving around the notes E, D and C, is indeed related to that of the oldest items in the repertoire, such as 'Lambango' and 'Sunjata', suggesting an origin on the balo (xylophone). Amadu Bansang begins his performances with either the Tilibo or the 'oldest' kumbengo, either of which may also recur at the end of a performance, while the other two seem to require introduction. The Malian kumbengo (Example 9)[23] is a relatively recent addition to his repertoire, having been taught to him by his nephew Sidiki Jobate (see section IV below) during a visit to The Gambia some years ago. Many young players from upper-river Gambia have also added it to their repertoire. Amadu Bansang does not usually spend long on this kumbengo and sometimes omits it altogether. In contrast, it is his own kumbengo to which he generally devotes the greatest amount of time, even though it is subject to little variation other than the alternation between duple and triple time (Example 9 (i)

19  See note 9.
20  E.g. in Knight 1973: vol. 2, p. 1; and on the Ethnodisc recording (see bibliography, Knight 1972), side 2 band 3.
21  Cf. no. 61.1 of Anthony King's unpublished transcriptions of the major items in the kora repertoire.
22  The basic melodic idea underlying the kumbengo; it may be established by treating all octaves, fifths and fourths as ornamentation. Where relevant, the melodic skeleton has been shown in the music examples.
23  Sometimes also called 'Yela'; cf. a performance of 'Tutu Jara' played by Sidiki Jobate and Batrou Kouyate which includes a version of 'Yela' as well as 'Segu Tutu': 'Première anthologie de la musique malienne: cordes anciennes' (Bärenreiter Musicaphon record BM 30 L 2505, side 1 band 1).

and (ii)). This kumbengo, which is not so far used by other musicians, appears to be derived from the 'key' phrase, which occurs four times in it.

The use of these four kumbengolu as a basis for performance makes Amadu Bansang's 'Tutu Jara' immediately distinctive. Even more characteristic are his variations. In performance, note patterns in 'Tutu Jara' and other pieces are subject to continual variation on a number of levels. The different types of variation, all of which are referred to as 'birimintingo', may be categorised broadly as:

(1) Variation based on the melodic idea inherent in the kumbengo. This type usually involves additional notes introduced either as passing notes[24] (stepwise movement being idiomatic to the kora because of the layout of the strings) or as 'kumbengo' notes, that is, octaves and fifths (or fourths). It may be seen from the music examples that Bs are generally followed by F♯s, As by Es, Ds by As, etc. These kumbengo notes may be played simultaneously as well as in succession. Variation on this level is usually present in the taught form of the recurrent theme;[25] elsewhere it may be applied randomly, or it may constitute a recurrent variation which is itself subject to further ornamentation.[26]

Example 4. (a) Ornamental formulas, which may begin on any note
(b) The typical 'Tutu Jara' ornamental phrase

(2) Variation departing from the kumbengo. This type of variation involves the substitution of a new phrase for part of the kumbengo, the phrase consisting of a new melodic motif[27] or a rapid ornamental passage.[28] Example 4 shows a few of the most common ornamental formulas in Amadu Bansang's style of playing, from which it can be seen that descending sequential pat-

24  E.g. the lower part of Example 6 (iii), played with the thumbs only.
25  Cf. Example 6 (i), the kumbengo as it is taught, with Example 6 (ii), a simplified version of the kumbengo heard in performance.
26  All the variations shown in the music examples are recurrent and may be heard on Eavadisc EDM 101 (see note 17), side 1 band 3, except for the Malian kumbengo, which is omitted from this performance.
27  As in the first half of Example 5 (ii) and (iii).
28  E.g. the first half of Example 9 (ii).

terns are predominant. While similar formulas are used as ornamentation in other pieces, their correct positioning, which is crucial to style, may differ for each kumbengo.[29] The square brackets in Examples 5–9 indicate the most common places for substituting new phrases in the 'Tutu Jara' kumbengolu. The 'key' phrase, however, may not be substituted except in the case of extended variations.

(3) Sariro variation. This is based on the technique called *sariro*, whereby two or three of the highest right- and left-hand strings are strummed with the fingers moving towards the player, while a simplified version of the melody is played with the thumbs. According to Amadu Bansang, sariro is used to make the kora sound louder at outdoor performances or in front of large audiences. There are only a few rhythmic patterns commonly used in sariro, and most of them involve cross-rhythms between fingers and thumbs, as in Example 6 (iv). It is significant that the melody played with the thumbs in this example corresponds exactly to the melodic skeleton as established for the Tilibo kumbengo, with which kumbengo the sariro is always associated in 'Tutu Jara'.

More extended variation (details of which are outside the scope of this study) is achieved by combining the techniques described, so that the resulting variation corresponds in length to two or more statements of the kumbengo (as in Example 7 (ii)). It is frequently made up of several isorhythmic ornamental phrases, which may also be sequential. Extended variations in 'Tutu Jara' should always return to the kumbengo with the 'key' phrase at the correct point in the tapped rhythmic pattern. In the context of vocal accompaniment, extended variations should take place only while the voice is silent. While some set variations may be attached to more than one kumbengo,[30] particularly where different kumbengolu share rhythmic characteristics, in general each set variation in 'Tutu Jara' is associated with only one theme.

From this study it may be seen that, although a kumbengo may be repeated with some consistency for teaching purposes, it should not be regarded as a fixed composition, or indeed as anything other than a melodic idea whose realisation into specific note patterns varies constantly from one player, and one performance, to another. While undoubtedly the kumbengo provides the musical framework, to describe a kora piece in terms of the kumbengo alone is insufficient; equally important are its associated variations and suitable places for inserting stock ornamental phrases. Detailed comparison between different musicians' performances may show that these aspects of kora music, too, are partly regional. In Amadu Bansang's style of playing, much of the variation in 'Tutu Jara' and other pieces is recurrent, while improvisation takes place within strictly defined limits and along formulaic lines. Finally, it may be observed that the use of more than one kumbengo as a basis for performance (which has hitherto gone unremarked) allows for a more extended structure and probably occurs primarily in instrumental solos.

29  Cf. Nyama Suso's phrase: 'good birimintingo depends on leaving and returning to the kumbengo smoothly', quoted by Knight (1973: 82).
30  E.g., Example 7 (i) may be followed by the variations shown in Example 5 (ii)–(iv).

Example 5. 'Tilibo' kumbengo, triple-time version

Melodic  skeleton:

Example 6. 'Tilibo' kumbengo, compound duple-time version

Melodic skeleton:

Example 7. Old kumbengo

Melodic skeleton:

(i)

N.B. damping of E optional

(ii)

Example 8. Amadu Bansang's kumbengo

(i)

(ii)

Example 9. Malian kumbengo

Melodic skeleton:

(i)

(ii)

## IV. Amadu Bansang Jobate: a biographical note

Amadu Bansang was born in Tambasansang (upper-river Gambia) sometime around the beginning of the First World War. His father, Jali Fili Jobate, who was originally from Kita in Mali,
settled in Tambasansang as musician to its first colonial ruler, Falai Kora. After Falai Kora's
death, rivalry over the colonial seat forced Jali Fili to look elsewhere for patronage and eventu-
ally he settled in Bansang (Macarthy Island Division), where Amadu spent his youth and hence
became known as 'Amadu Bansang'.

    Jali Fili was himself a kontingo player, though on settling in The Gambia he also took up the
kora since in that country it was the more favoured instrument. His repertoire and style on the
kora, however, were largely drawn from the kontingo. Amadu Bansang received his earliest
instruction from his father and later from his elder brother, Bala Jobate (the father of Sidiki
Jobate, now one of the leading players in the Mali National Ensemble). When Amadu was
roughly twenty-five years old he left Bansang for the Kombos, where he spent a number of years
with the Chiefs of Yeseu and Bakau, finally settling under the patronage of a wealthy trader
from Gunjur. On the latter's death he devoted himself exclusively to Koranic study for a period
of six years, following which he came under the patronage of Sanyali Bojang (the present Chief
of Brikama), with whom he has now been for some twenty years, for most of this time in
association with the singer Bamba Suso.

### Bibliography

Durán, L. 1978a. 'Kelefa Saane: the music', in Gordon Innes: *Kelefa Saane: his career recounted
    by two Mandinka bards*, London
Durán, L. 1978b. 'The Mandinka kora', *Recorded Sound* no. 69, p. 754
Durán, L. 1979. 'Amadu Bansang Jobarteh: master of the kora', booklet accompanying Eavadisc
    record EDM 101, Cambridge
King, Anthony 1972. 'The construction and tuning of the *kora*', *African Language Studies* XIII,
    pp. 113f.
King, Anthony 1974. 'Music: the performance modes', in Gordon Innes: *Sunjata, three Man-
    dinka versions*, London, pp. 17f.
Knight, Roderic 1971. 'Towards a notation and tablature for the *kora*', *African Music* V part 1,
    pp. 23f.
Knight, Roderic 1972. 'Kora Manding: Mandinka music of The Gambia', booklet accompanying
    Ethnodisc record ER 12102
Knight, Roderic 1973. 'Mandinka Jaliya: professional music of The Gambia', 2 vols., unpub-
    lished Ph.D. dissertation, University of California, Los Angeles
Park, Mungo 1799. *Travels in the interior districts of West Africa*, London

# A Sogdian friction-chordophone

HARVEY TURNBULL

In 1965 Laurence Picken[1] examined the earliest (eighth century A.D.) Chinese reference to the excitation of the strings of a musical instrument by friction. The instrument in question, the yazheng, was a half-tube zither (zheng), the element *ya* 札 indicating that a stick without hair was used to sound the strings. The reference, in the *Jiu Tangshu* ('Old Tang History'), runs: 'The yazheng is made to creak (*ya*) with a slip of bamboo, moistened at its tip.' There are no known contemporary illustrations of the yazheng, but a woodcut of it appears in the 1876 edition of the *Yüeshu* by Cheng Yang (preface dated 1104), where the slip of bamboo appears as 'an L-shaped object, with the longer leg of the L about five times the length of the shorter leg' (Picken 1965). The 1195 edition of the *Yüeshu*, as well as repeating the description of the yazheng found in the *Jiu Tangshu*, also contains the first Chinese reference to a friction-chordophone of the lute class, the xiqin, an instrument of foreign origin: 'the two strings are made to creak by a slip of bamboo between them'. Mention is also made in the *Yüeshu* of the huqin, again an instrument of foreign origin. In Tang times the huqin was a finger-plucked lute. Structural details are lacking until the *Yuanshi* (the official history of the Yuan dynasty, completed in 1370), where it is compared with the hobisi/huobusi (Turkic kobuz); it had two strings and was played with a horsehair bow. The *Yuanshi* compares the huobusi to the piba: it had a straight fretless neck, a small trough-shaped, circular, skin-covered belly, and four strings, while the piba had frets, was made of wood, and was broad.

Bachmann's researches into the origins of bowing led him to the conclusion that the probable site of the first use of the bow is to be located in Central Asia. As well as the Chinese evidence, Bachmann (like Picken) quotes Al-Fārābi's observation (tenth century A.D.) on certain instruments 'the strings of which are made to sound by rubbing them with other strings, or with something similar'. Bachmann's conclusion is that 'on the evidence of the sources, Central Asia may be regarded as the birthplace of bowing; the use of the friction-stick in this region before the tenth century can be demonstrated with a high degree of probability; and the first

I am most grateful to Dr A. Ivanov of the State Hermitage, Leningrad, for his invaluable assistance in obtaining information about, and photographs of, archaeological finds of organological interest in Central Asia.

1  Picken 1965; the Chinese evidence summarised here is drawn from this paper. See also Wolpert 1974.

197

Figure 1. Detail from the Airtam frieze (Leningrad, The Hermitage)

mention of a horsehair bow, early in the tenth century, also refers to Central Asia. We may assume from Al-Fārābi's description that in the tenth century " other similar implements" apart from the bow were employed to excite the strings of Central Asian chordophones' (1969: 55).

Half-tube zithers have remained confined to the Far Eastern instrumentarium, and, although the use of a friction-stick on the zither is reported earlier than its use on a lute, it is probable that the practice of playing zithers in this way arose in imitation of friction-played lutes. The early representations of zithers in China are finger-plucked, whereas lutes, both in China and in Central Asia, were played either with the fingers or with a plectrum, and the transition from plectrum to friction-stick is more likely to have come about in practice than the transition from fingers to friction-stick. Examination of the lutes of pre-mediaeval Central Asia and China reveals an extremely wide range of instrument types and methods of performance. For the present study, concentration will be on the means of sound production, in particular the variety of plectra.

The earliest representation of a long-necked lute in Central Asia appears on a rhyton discovered at Nisa[2] (eight miles from Ashkhabad), where the Parthian kings built their palaces and temples; the rhytons found there date from the second to the first century B.C. Artistically linked with the finds at Nisa is the sculpture discovered at Khalchayan (first century B.C.), a

2  See Masson and Pugachenkova 1956: pl. LXXX.

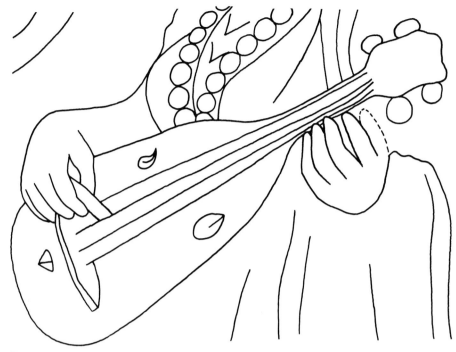

Figure 2. Detail of a relief at Taxila (Rome, Museo d'Arte Orientale)

site in southern Uzbekistan. A fragment from a frieze shows a girl playing a lute (see Pugachen-kova 1966: Fig. 1); although only part of the instrument remains (half of the body, with the beginning of a tapering neck) it is clearly a short-necked lute, the earliest of its type in Central Asia. On the table can be made out a broad bridge, with the beginnings of two strings; these are sufficiently widely spaced to be the top and bottom strings of a four-stringed instrument. A waisted lute from the following century appears in a similar frieze found at nearby Airtam (see Prynne 1955: pl. VI). The plectrum is clearly visible in this representation, and is typical of those used on other early Central Asian lutes. It is short, about seven centimetres in length, and about finger width. Generally plectra are held between thumb and finger tips. The hand approaches the strings sometimes from below, as in the Airtam frieze (see Figure 1), sometimes from above (Figure 2), while in some cases the approach is from below the bridge, with the forearm parallel to the strings (Figure 3). The performer is generally shown standing, with the instrument held high, the back resting against the player's body. Support of the instrument in this playing position is completed by the right forearm resting on the rim of the table, with the left hand holding the neck. This method of holding the instrument severely restricts movement. However, because of the shortness of the plectrum, it is possible to activate it by wrist rotation when the forearm is parallel to the strings (Figure 3), and by a combination of hand and finger movement when the forearm is at right angles to the strings (Figures 1, 2); in both cases the wrist can be sufficiently arched to allow the tip of the plectrum to strike the strings without the forearm losing contact with the instrument and withdrawing its support.

Figure 3. Terracotta figurine at Afrāsiyāb site,
Samarkand (after Sir Marc Aurel Stein, *Ancient
Khotan* (Oxford 1907), pl. LXXXVIII)

Figure 4. Detail of a relief at Gong xian
(in modern Honan Province)

The diffusion of these early lute types can be traced in the many representations of musicians featured in terracottas, sculpture and wall-paintings. Works of art inspired by Buddhism are rich in musical iconography, and between the turn of the millennium and mediaeval times many instrument types are depicted. Some time before the fifth century A.D., Buddhism took firm root in China, and monuments to the new faith began to appear. The main passage of influence was through Central Asia to northern China; it is here that a number of Buddhist centres arose, and with them appeared cave-temples, a type of structure that originated in India and spread to Afghanistan, Central Asia and China.

In the Buddhist cave-temples of northern China, representations of musicians are plentiful. Lutes of different types are in evidence, and particularly noticeable is the appearance of new types of plectra. The caves at Yungang, near Datong in the north of modern Shansi Province, were begun in the second half of the fifth century. Generally the lute players depicted here use a plectrum similar to those occurring earlier in Central Asia. In one or two cases, however, the plectrum appears to be rectangular in shape, and quite broad; such a plectrum can be seen in Cave VI, which dates from the end of the century, together with a plectrum of the more usual type.[3] With such a broad plectrum, it is logical to assume that the corner was used to strike the strings.

3   See Mizuno and Nagahiro 1952–6: vol. III, part I, Pl. 50.

At Gong xian in modern Honan Province, further development is evident. The sculptures here are in the style typical of the end of the Northern Wei dynasty (386–535). The early sixth-century lutenists at Gong xian[4] used plectra very much longer than those so far considered; they appear to be at least twenty centimetres long and are held by the middle, with the lower part projecting below the players' hands. The shapes vary; the slimmer plectra have the long sides parallel, while the broader plectra exhibit a slight taper. The larger plectra appear to be about four to five centimetres wide, and the broad face is presented to the strings, with the long axis at right angles to them. Two of the lutenists in particular call for comment. One[5] is playing a piba-type lute of large dimensions, with a long narrow plectrum (see Figure 4). He is shown sitting cross-legged, with the lute resting in his lap; this is remarkable, as, even when lutenists were shown seated, they normally retained the high playing position, with the instrument resting on the chest. This is the playing position adopted by the other lutenist,[6] who plays a round-

Figure 5. Detail of a relief at Gong xian

bodied, long-necked lute with a broad plectrum (see Figure 5). The first lutenist grips the plectrum with all the fingers and the thumb, which lies along the long side of the plectrum at right angles to the fingers. The second lutenist holds his broad plectrum between the tips of the thumb and all the fingers; his wrist is arched, which brings the hand into position for a down-stroke. These details suggest new styles of performance. By supporting the lute on his legs, the

4  *Gong xian shiku shi*: pls. 41, 61, 134 and 235.
5  *Ibid.*: pl. 235.
6  *Ibid.*: pl. 61.

first player frees the right arm from its support of the instrument. The greater movement that this allows would enable him to sweep through all the strings with the long plectrum; such a vigorous stroke would be supported by the firmer grip. The second lutenist, who holds the long, broad plectrum rather delicately, would not be able to achieve such a movement; he is restricted to a turn of the wrist, which would cause the plectrum to *rub* over the strings.

There is both literary and iconographic evidence in support of the long plectrum being regarded as a means of producing a stroke through all the strings, similar to that used on the Japanese biwa in the performance of Gagaku (Japanese court music). The tenth-century *Yuefu zalu* refers to piba performers in the Zhenyuan era (785–804) producing sounds like thunder, wind, and rain; Gimm comments on the use of a powerful stroke of the large wooden plectrum to produce such sounds, and compares this technique with the more delicate finger style of performance, dating from the seventh century.[7] Representations of lute-players in the Tang period (618–906) reveal that the wooden table of the instrument was protected from the heavy plectrum strokes by a guard, a wide strip of leather fixed across the table.

During the Tang period further developments took place in the plectrum. The handle became slimmer, while the upper part flared out considerably into a fan shape. This very elegant design was perhaps the result of functional needs. The slimmer handle would have made the plectrum more comfortable to hold, while the flared upper blade would have made it more efficient in the context of the restrictions imposed on the hand when the lute is held high. The pronounced curvature of the flared blade produces projections at right angles to the longitudinal axis of the plectrum; this provides easier access to the strings when the hand is near the table. Indeed, in some representations the player's hand is *between* the plectrum and the strings, with the palm facing away from the player, the reverse of the overhand grip[8] (see Figure 6).

The corpus of surviving Tang lute music includes one source that provides a list of twenty-eight tunings, two of which have the lowest two strings in unison. The music in this collection excludes the use of a plectrum.[9] It is difficult to see the reason for such doubling in the tuning of the main strings of an instrument where the strings are plucked individually by the fingers. It does make sense, however, when all the strings are sounded together by rubbing with a friction-stick, or by a sweep of a plectrum; in the former case sounds would be reinforced,[10] while in both cases they would be concordant, particularly with the second tuning, where the intervallic structure of key-note, fifth and octave occurs on modern Central Asian lutes, and was a tuning used for bowed instruments in mediaeval Europe (Bachmann 1969: 54). It will be recalled that the description of the huobusi in the *Yuanshi* included mention of four strings. Modern Central Asian instruments of the kobuz type have been reported with two or three strings.[11] If the *Yuanshi* is not mistaken in attributing four strings to the instrument, it appears likely that this was an arrangement of two paired strings, as the huobusi is compared with the two-stringed

---

7   Gimm 1966: 308, 309 and 379 (A138).
8   See Binyon and Stein 1921: pl. XXXVIII; also Sickman and Soper 1971: Fig. 156.
9   See Wolpert 1977: 131–2 (tables of tunings) and 151.
10  Bachmann mentions unfavourable Muslim reports on 'the bowed instrument's thin, unat-
    tractive tone' (1969: 55).
11  Bachmann 1969: 48; Chadwick and Zhirmunsky 1969: 25.

Figure 6. Detail of a tenth-century painting on silk: 'Night Entertainment of Han Xizai', by Gu Hongzhong (Peking, Palace Museum)

huqin. Unison tuning of the two upper strings in the above piba tunings would have reinforced the treble sounds, as was done in mediaeval Europe (Bachmann 1969: 48); one wonders if such a step was ever taken in China.

The question arises whether the long plectrum originated in China or was an import. It appeared during the sixth century, a time when Central Asian influence was strong. The profound effect of Buddhism has already been mentioned; foreign musics had also been well received, and by the Sui dynasty (581–618) had become firmly established. Among those listed in the *Suishu* ('Sui History') and both *Tangshu* ('Tang Histories') are several from Central Asian regions, including Kutcha, Kashgar and Samarkand (Liu 1958: 199f).

A funerary monument found at Zhangde fu, near Anyang in northern Honan Province, is decorated with reliefs depicting scenes that are quite un-Chinese in character. Stylistically they are related to the cave sculptures at the Xiangtang temple (550–77). Among the musicians on the Zhangde fu reliefs are several lutenists, some of whom employ long plectra. These are much slimmer than the plectra at Gong xian, and they are only slightly flared. Scaglia[12] has concluded that the source for this monument lay in the region of Samarkand, which was also the provenance of the persons depicted in the ceremony. This finding has been confirmed as a result of archaeological discoveries made in the Samarkand area at Pendzhikent, the capital of a small principality in ancient Sogdia (see Belenitsky and Marshak 1971: 20).

Sogdian iconography[13] includes representations of two lute-players. One of these appears in a wall-painting dating from the sixth century. The painting is in urgent need of restoration, and to see all the details the careful sketch made by P.I. Kostrov at the time of discovery must be consulted (Plate 1). The female musician holds a piba-type lute pointing downwards. The stick in her right hand is broad at the head and tapers to a thinner lower section held in the hand and projecting below it. The stick is even longer than the long plectra in the Chinese representations.

12  Scaglia 1958: 27; the lutenists can be seen in Fig. 3.
13  For a survey of Sogdian instruments see Bentovich 1976.

Plate 1. Sketch by P.I. Kostrov of a Sogdian wall-painting, made at the time of its discovery (courtesy of the State Hermitage, Leningrad)

The hand is over the lower rim of the instrument, and the stick projects above it about seventeen or eighteen centimetres; in all it must have been some thirty centimetres long (these estimates are based on a modern piba similar in size, relative to the human body, to the instrument shown).

Belenitsky (1961: 91) described the object as 'a short bow'. Vyzgo (1972: 288) has argued against this view: 'it is too short to be a bow, and it is devoid of the characteristics of a bow; secondly, the form of the instrument is characteristic of the lute class'. In a footnote Vyzgo cites the opinion of A.I. Petrosyantz that 'the musician holds the object not as a bow, but as a plectrum; on an instrument of such width and form it is impossible to play with a bow otherwise than simultaneously on all four strings'. Vyzgo also suggests the possibility that the drawing may be inaccurate.

Sufficient detail is discernible in a photograph of the original painting to discount the suggestion of inaccuracy in the sketch, if it is a question of the length of the stick. The part of the stick that projects below the player's hand can be made out, and in order to reach the strings, the stick must have been of a length similar to that shown in the sketch. A short plectrum can be ruled out as the forearm is used to support the instrument (again, this can be seen in the original), and if the hand was carried nearer the strings the instrument would overbalance.

The assumptions made by Vyzgo and Petrosyantz that lutes of this form are not bowed, and that bowing cannot take place on all strings simultaneously, are invalidated by an instrument of similar shape to the Sogdian lute in an eleventh-century Byzantine fresco in Kiev (Bachmann 1969: pl. 8); it is undoubtedly bowed, and the plane of the six strings is flat.

The limitation of arm movement on the Sogdian lute implies that it would not have been possible to pluck the strings with the end of the stick in plectrum style. The movement that is possible, rotation of the wrist, allows the hand sufficient freedom to move the stick a short way up and down. As the face of the stick is in the same plane as that of the strings, this entails that the end section of the stick would have rubbed backwards and forwards on the strings.[14] The only alternative movement is a turn of the hand, in which case the stick could have been used as a beater. Against this is the fact that the wrist is shown to be arched, with the hand ready to draw the stick across the strings. The natural position for a beating action is to have the hand, wrist and forearm in line.

While the object can therefore be plausibly identified as a friction-stick, the question of whether it can be regarded as a bow must be left open. The answer depends on the interpretation given to details in the sketch that are of considerable interest but which have as yet aroused no comment: these are (a) the curvature in the stick below the player's hand; (b) the rectangular section at the upper end of the stick; (c) the detail at the lower end.

(a) The curvature is such that the lower termination point is below the longitudinal axis of the straight upper portion of the stick; this means that a line between the two ends would pass below the player's fingers.

(b) The rectangular section may indicate (i) merely that the upper part of the stick is rectangular in cross-section, or (ii) that a separate attachment, or carved extension, is set at right angles to the stick. In the case of (ii), this would allow the hair to be separated from the straight section of the stick in the area of contact with the strings.

(c) There appears to be an integral knob at the lower end of the stick; this would allow the attachment of strands of hair.

Given (a), (b) (ii) and (c), then all the conditions necessary for the object's being a bow are satisfied. It differs from the many representations of bows in later mediaeval illustrations, in which the stick has the shape of a simple archer's bow, curved along the entire length between the points of attachment of the hair. However, if the object with the Sogdian lute is accepted as a bow, then it is an excellent illustration of the modifications necessary in adapting a friction-stick, essentially straight, to allow the attachment of horsehair.

The conclusions to be drawn are that friction-sticks were first used on lutes in Sogdia in or before the sixth century; this technique was transmitted to China, where the long stick influenced

14   The fact that only the end of the stick rubs across the strings helps to explain why the slip of bamboo used to play the yazheng was 'moistened at its tip', and further supports the view that friction-sticks on lutes preceded friction-sticks on zithers. Early representations of plucked zithers in China show the instrument resting either on the ground or on the player's legs. It is therefore surprising that the full length of the stick was not used, as in modern performance on, for example, the Korean ajaeng (featured in a filmed performance of 'Sujech'ŏn', *Traditional Korean music and dance*, produced by Harvey Turnbull, AVT/KOR/2, Ethnomusicological Audio Visual Archive, University of Cambridge).

plectrum-style playing, producing the large flared plectra used in one style of Tang lute perform-ance; in China the technique of sounding the strings by friction was also applied to the zither (zheng). That influence was not all one way is suggested by the second lute in the representations of Sogdian instruments. This appears in a later wall-painting dating from the eighth century, which includes musicians playing an arched harp and pan-pipes (Belenitsky 1959: pl. XI). The painting is badly damaged with parts missing, but sufficient remains of the lute to establish that it had a plectrum guard (cf. p. 202). To the writer's knowledge this is the only representation of such a lute in this area of Central Asia.

## Bibliography

Bachmann, W. 1969. *The origins of bowing*, London
Bentovich, I.B. 1976. 'Muzykal'nye Instrumenty Drevnego Sogda', *Ordena Trudovogo Znameni Institut Arkheologii, Kratkie Soobshcheniya* 147, Moscow
Binyon, L. and Stein, Sir Marc Aurel 1921. *The Thousand Buddhas: ancient Buddhist paintings from the cave-temples of Tun-huang on the western frontier of China*, London
Belenitsky, A.M. 1959. 'Novye Pamyatniki Iskusstva Drevnego Penzhikenta', *Skul'ptura i Zhivopis Drevnego Pendzhikenta*, Moscow
Belenitsky, A.M. 1961. 'Ob arkheologicheskikh rabotakh Pyanzhikentskogo otryada v 1958g.', *Trudy Instituta Istorii im. Akhmada Donisha* XXVI, Tashkent
Belenitsky, A.M. and Marshak, B.I. 1971. 'L'art de Piandjikent à la lumière des dernières fouilles (1958–1968)', *Arts Asiatiques* XXIII
Gimm, M. 1966. *Das Yüeh-fu tsa-lu des Tuan An-chieh*, Wiesbaden
*Gong xian shiku shi* 鞏縣石窟寺, Peking 1963
Liu Mau-Tsai 1958. 'Kulturelle Baziehungen zwischen den Ost-Türken (= T'u-küe) und China', *Central Asiatic Journal* III no. 3
Masson, M.E. and Pugachenkova, G.A. 1956. *Parfyanskie Ritony Nisy iz Kul'turnogo Naslediya Turkmenskogo Naroda: Al'bom Illustratsii*, Moscow
Mizuno, S. and Nagahiro, T. 1952–6. *Yün-kang, the Buddhist cave temples of the fifth century A.D. in North China*, 16 vols., Kyoto
Picken, L.E.R. 1965. 'Early Chinese friction-chordophones', *Galpin Society Journal* XVIII
Prynne, M. 1955. 'Angelic musicians from Central Asia', *Galpin Society Journal* VIII
Pugachenkova, G.A. 1966. 'Devushka s lyutnei v skul'pture Khalchayana', *Kul'tura Antichnogo Mira*, Moscow
Scaglia, G. 1958. 'Central Asians on a Northern Ch'i gate shrine', *Artibus Asiae* XXI
Sickman, L. and Soper, A. 1971. *The art and architecture of China*, Harmondsworth
Vyzgo, T.S. 1972. 'Afrasiabskaya lyutnya', *Iz Istorii Iskusstva Velikogo Goroda*, ed. G.A. Pugachenkova, Tashkent
Wolpert, R.F. 1974. 'Einige Bemerkungen zur Geschichte des Streichinstruments in China', *Central Asiatic Journal* XVIII no. 4
Wolpert, R.F. 1977. 'A ninth-century Sino-Japanese lute-tutor', *Musica Asiatica* I, Oxford

**Glossary**

ajaeng 牙箏
Chen Yang 陳暘
hobisi/huobusi 火不思
huqin (hu-ch'in) 胡琴
piba (p'i-p'a) 琵琶
xiqin (hsi ch'in) 溪琴
yazheng (ya chêng) 軋箏
Yuefu zalu (Yüeh-fu tsa-lu) 樂府雜錄
Yueshu (Yüeh Shu) 樂書

# The iconography of arched harps in Burma

MURIEL C. WILLIAMSON

The modern Burmese harp
Predella from Léyindaung hill, Śrī Kṣetra (mid seventh century)
Paunggu Temple relief (A.D. *c.* 1050)
West Hpetleik Guttila-plaque (A.D. *c.* 1070)
Shwézigôn Guttila-plaque (A.D. *c.* 1086)
Nagayôn predellas (A.D. *c.* 1090)
Predellas of the Nanda Temple (A.D. *c.* 1105)
Lokahteikpan Temi Jâtaka (A.D. 1113–*c.* 1155)
Later developments

These notes first took shape in a letter of appreciation to Professor G.H. Luce in 1972, describing representations of harps that I had found in his monumental work *Old Burma – Early Pagán*

---

1   In this study 'Burma' refers to the geographical area we know as modern Burma. 'Burmese'
    refers to the people of Tangut Lolo stock who originally came from the northwest of China
    and finally descended into the central plain as late as the ninth century A.D. They founded
    Pagán, it is said, in A.D. *c.* 850; it was sacked by the Mongols in A.D. 1287. The Pyu
    descended from the northeast and established their great city of Śrī Kṣetra in A.D. 638,
    but were forced to retire to their northern capital of Halin in the eighth century, where
    they were annihilated in A.D. 832. The Mon, basically a people of the tropic delta, arrived
    centuries earlier after a long migration, mostly from the Hanoi area. 'Old Burmese', the
    early language of the Burmans, 'is close to Tibetan and Archaic Chinese languages, and
    quite unconnected with "Old Mon", apart from common borrowings from Sanskrit/Pali'
    (letter from Professor Luce, 27 August 1972).
        I am specifically indebted and feel deeply grateful to the following persons: G.H. Luce,
    who has answered all of my questions; Laurence Picken, who will be surprised to see his
    translation; John Okell, for linguistic assistance in Old Burmese; Roy Craven, Director of
    the University of Florida Gallery, who read the paper from an artist's point of view; Jane
    Terry Bailey, Professor of Burmese Art at Denison University, who confirmed dates and
    styles; Paul Fox of the School of Oriental and African Studies, University of London, and
    also the University of Florida Instructional Resources Center, for photographic assistance;
    John Byron, for examining the Victoria and Albert Museum harp; and, not the least,
    Richard Widdess, my harp pupil, whose advice on format made the work easier to undertake.

Plate 1. The modern Burmese harp, played by Daw Khin Khin Galè (1883–1961)

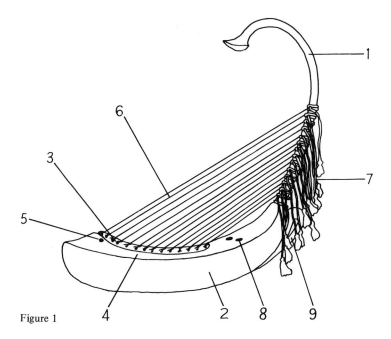

Figure 1

(vols. I–III, 1969–70). Laurence Picken, on reading those notes later, suggested that they be revised for publication. The resulting study is now tendered in recognition of Dr Picken's own valuable contributions in the field of Asian musicology.

The arched harp is generally thought to have originated in Mesopotamia *c.* 3000 B.C. (Williamson 1969). Its eastward 'migration' is represented in the iconography of ancient India by the vinā, associated with Buddhist courts from *c.* 200 B.C. to the seventh century A.D. (Marcel-Dubois 1941: 80–6, 115 and 139), by which time it was already present in Lower Burma at the Pyu capital of Śrī Ksetra (Becker 1967: 17–23 and pl. V–VII). In Burma it still exists, both in its sophisticated court style, tuned by cords encircling the arch, and in more remote tribal types usually tuned by pegs.

The present study deals with the evolution of the arched harp in Burma as seen in a chronological presentation of the published iconography. Certain features of the construction, the playing position, and the playing technique of the modern harp (*c.* 1960: Williamson 1968) will be used as a standard of comparison for the earlier examples.

### The modern Burmese harp (saùng-gauk)

The structure of the modern harp (see Figure 1) includes the following parts: (1) A slender tapered arch made of cutch root that curves outward at the base and recurves at the top, so that its flared terminal, in the shape of a *bo*-tree leaf, hangs well back over the harp. The arch is roughly equal in overall height to the length of the resonator. It may have either of two traditional shapes, 'orchid spray' or 'monkey seat', of which the latter rises more directly upwards. (2) A boat-shaped resonator hollowed from *padauk* heartwood, with a cup-shaped stern and high prow, into which the arch is deeply embedded. (3) A string-bar, with fourteen holes drilled in its concave mid-section and a convex hump at the rear, is threaded through two slits in (4) the deer-skin table of the resonator, so that the mid-section rests on top of the skin, and extremities are attached to the resonator underneath the skin. When stretched tightly and nailed to the lip of the resonator, the skin covers the convexity at the rear of the string-bar to form a hump called the 'monkey head' (5). (6) Fourteen strings are tied to the string-bar, and attached to the arch by means of tuning cords with long tasselled ends (7). Four sound-holes are cut in the skin (8). (9) A highly decorated wooden loop (*hsahtò*), unique to the Burmese harp, protrudes from the prow of the resonator below the arch. This may be placed under the left knee during tuning, to brace the instrument. The harp is decorated with red and black lacquer, and embellished with gold leaf.

The harpist sits cross-legged, or with feet tucked backward to the side (see Plate 1). The harp is balanced slantwise across the lap so that the prow, tilted slightly down, rests near the left knee, the mid-section across the right thigh and against the hip under the right elbow, the 'monkey head' extending beyond the elbow. In this position the strings are not quite horizontal but rise to the arch at an angle of approximately $20°$, though this varies somewhat among individual harpists.

The left hand operates on the 'inside' surface of the strings, nearest the player. The tip of the left forefinger often rests on the top string, or on the inside of the arch, while the arch itself is balanced against the third and fourth fingers on its outer side. The whole hand is poised to move agilely down and up the arch for the purpose of stopping strings with the thumb-nail, to obtain pitches in addition to those of the gapped tuning. The left thumb may also pluck strings from the inside in order to provide a drone tone or to double an octave. The strings are activated (stroked or plucked) on the 'outside' surface at the centre of their length, either singly or two together, with the calloused forefinger and thumb of the right hand. To avoid dissonance the third finger may damp one string as the forefinger plays the next.

## Predella[2] from Léyindaung hill, Śrī Kṣetra (mid seventh century): see Figure 2

This predella was published and described by Judith Becker in 1967. It pushes back harp-history in Burma a century and a half before the earliest literary documentation, by Tang-dynasty Chinese historians in the *Xin Tangshu* (C 222). In that account a large and a small harp were included in the description of musical instruments of the Pyu orchestra that performed for

---

2  The term 'predella' is used for the panel carved in relief beneath a seated Buddha, to represent a relevant scene from the life of Gotama, or a Jātaka-scene illustrating one of Gotama's 550 former existences. Such reliefs were used to educate the people in the religion. This predella appears in the Archaeological Survey of India Annual Report for 1927–8, p. 132; photographic negative 3002.

the Tang Emperor in A.D. 802. In the predella seven figures (the far left one vestigial) are centred in the foreground by a lively dancer, accompanied by three musicians playing (from left to right) an arched harp, large (possibly bamboo) clappers, and a small wind instrument (could this be the now obsolete hnyin, a mouth-organ?). The crowned Bodhissatva is seated in *dhyānamudrā* on the right, with a female figure on his left. Though Luce (1969, I: 146) describes this scene, with some doubt, as Indra's visit to Gotama at Indasāla Cave accompanied by Pañca-sikha playing his harp, the presence of the dancer and musicians together with the female figure (Māra's daughter?) might well depict the Temptation of Gotama.

Through the veil of erosion only an impression remains of the structure of this small harp. The arch was shaped with care and seems to have been slender and graceful. It leaves the resonator at an angle of approximately 110°, rises upward in 'monkey seat' shape (rather than 'orchid spray') to the level of the harpist's ear, where it recurves sharply and terminates in a scroll. The height of the arch is comparable to the length of the resonator, which may have protruded somewhat beyond the harpist's elbow. There may have been four or five strings, indicated vaguely by a few diagonal shadows on the chest of the player, and perhaps vestiges of cords or pegs above and below the bulge on the arch.

The harpist sits cross-legged, the resonator supported above his waist-band against his chest. The resonator is almost obscured by the right arm, elbow and enormous hand, which help to support the harp. The equally large left hand seems to be grasping the arch about half-way up, from the inside. The string shadows are close to 40° from horizontal, owing partly to the horizontal position of the resonator, whereas the string-angle of the modern harp in playing position is only 20° from horizontal.

Figure 2                                              Figure 3

- - - = indistinct          · · · = conjectural

The clearly defined thumb and forefinger of the right hand lie close to the site of the shortest diagonal string-shadow, ready to pluck on the outside surface of the strings, as in modern practice.

I agree with Becker (1967) that the whole scene represented here has a certain indigenous quality about it, as though taken from real life. She relates this harp to the smaller type described in the *Xin Tangshu*, and (dispensing with the Pagán harps altogether) links it directly to the modern harp (Becker 1967: 23). However, a fresh translation by Dr Picken of the ambiguous passage in the *Xin Tangshu* concerning the smaller harp suggests that it might be translated: 'The other one had long tuning-pegs on the neck.'[3] This does not agree very well with the tuning cords characteristic of the modern harp: it suggests rather the Karen harp with pegs, described by T. Stern and T.A. Stern (1971: 187).

### Paunggu Temple relief (A.D. *c.* 1050): see **Figure 3**[4]

In the Pagán Museum a series of figures in stone relief includes seven musicians playing harp, clapper, cymbals, drum and small wind instruments. They were recovered from Paunggu Temple before the Irawady finally washed it away. The temple was first attributed to Kyanzittha, and later to Aniruddha (Anorahtā) (A.D. 1044—77). In 1915 Duroiselle, then in charge, thought these reliefs to be copies of Indian sculptures. Luce states, however, that though artists in Burma often adopted Indian motifs they always treated them in their own strongly native style — a view confirmed here by facial type, headdress, clothing and musical instruments.

This harpist was first described by Luce as a standing figure 'clapping hands'; he has since acknowledged my interpretation.[5] The arch of the harp is faintly recognisable as it rises from the grasp of the player's left hand: it terminates under his chin. Fragments of the right forearm and resonator still exist in spite of mutilation, protruding beneath the right and left hand-positions. The strings, perhaps originally numbering five or more, rise at an angle of 45° from horizontal.

Though standing harpists occur in India, and at least once on the Bayon at Angkor Thom (Morton 1976: fig. 11), this is the only example known to me in Burma. In India, harps played in this fashion were supported at waist level by a sling (Marcel-Dubois 1941: 84), the Khmer harp by the left arm; but here the left hand and arm seem to be used to support the instrument on the outside, in exactly the position used by the Mari harpists in Mesopotamia, 2700 B.C. (Williamson 1969: fig. 2).

The right hand is mutilated by a deep gouge at the centre, but could have been in position to play in the centre of the outside surface of the strings, as in modern practice.

This harp may be related to the Pyu harp of Śrī Kṣetra. Since Pyu bronze Buddhas were

3  Letter from Dr Picken, 8 August 1973 (*Xin Tangshu* C 222).
4  Luce 1970, III: pl. 153d; 1969, I: pp. 294—6. Also Archaeological Survey of India 1915—16; photo neg. 1538. Size 5½ by 3½ inches.
5  Luce 1969, II: 96. Letter from Professor Luce, 17 April 1972.

Figure 4

found at the same site, Pyu as well as South Indian influences were present here. The head-dresses seen in the Pyu predella and those worn by the other Paunggu musicians, as well as faces with similar features in both reliefs, are very like those of the Pyu stela discovered in 1929 at their later capital of Halingyi, near Shwebo in Upper Burma (Le May 1954/6: 47 and fig. 2). The harpist is accompanied by a clapper-player immediately at his left, as in the Śrī Ksetra predella.

## West Hpetleik Guttila-plaque (A.D. *c.* 1070): see Figure 4[6]

Three miles south of the walled city, Aniruddha encased two older pagodas and added circum-ambulatory corridors with three tiers of unglazed terracotta plaques illustrating the 550 Jātaka. Each plaque is inscribed with its name and number in the elegant early Mon script used by him. They are thought to be the work of Mon artisans brought to Pagán after the conquest of Thaton in A.D. 1057. This art may stem from an indigenous wood-carving craft, or it may carry a much older artistic tradition of the coastal area, perhaps inherited from Indian sculptors from Kalinga (Luce 1969, I: 267). Jātaka 243 describes the contest between the royal harpist (and Bodhis-satva) Guttila and his pupil Mūsila (representing Devadatta), who has challenged his master's position as court harpist. In this scene Guttila and Mūsila play before the king. Guttila, follow-ing the advice of Sakka (possibly seated above, playing a third and smaller harp), breaks one

6   Luce 1970, III: pl. 101a; 1969, I: pp. 262–7. Plaques 15 inches square.

string after another until no strings are left; whereupon he continues to play so beautifully that he wins the competition, thus proving the miraculous quality of his musicianship.

Though too much weathered to reveal details of structure, the harps of Guttila and Mūsila have an overall crescent-shaped contour. They are large, with substantial arches that rise above the heads of the harpists. The terminals do not project far beyond string attachments; the resonators are boat-shaped with high prows and shallow cup-like sterns (perhaps forerunners of the modern harp in this respect). It is hard to tell just where the arch leaves the body, but it is probably at half the span of the overall crescent. In the modern harp this shape would be called 'orchid spray', with a smooth curve of about $170°$ at the juncture. The strings are somewhat individuated in the larger harp, and are attached high on the arch, in the manner of the bird-headed Khmer harps carved in relief on the outer gallery of the Bayon at Angkor Thom (negative reversed in Morton 1976: fig. 14; see Groslier 1957: pl. 168–70). Here, however, a number of encircling strictures are faintly visible on the arches, especially noticeable on the larger harp. These perhaps indicate tuning cords (rather than pegs) though there are no tassels. A row of holes along the surface or table of the resonator in Guttila's harp (left) and more widely spaced holes in the same position on that of Mūsila (right) should not, in my opinion, be interpreted unequivocally as string holes, because there is no particular alignment with what few strings are vaguely individuated (in Mūsila's harp only). There is an erosion of the whole fabric of the plaque so that the original unglazed facing is largely missing. Many more such perforations are scattered over the present surface, especially in the deeper layers of the relief, including the heavenly area to the right of Sakka.

The third harp above – played by the figure who may be meant to represent Sakka – is of a different type. The god in heaven and his harp are on a smaller scale. He may be sitting in Buddha-position on a mat. The scoop-shaped resonator is short in proportion to the arch, which appears to be gracefully recurved and tapered, rising to the level of the brow. The general aspect may be likened to the Pyu, Paunggu, or modern harps, rather than to the crescent-shaped harps below it. Strings and other details are not clearly visible, however.

The harpists Guttila and Mūsila sit in a position typical of Pagán, with feet tucked under, both knees showing in front. Here they are placed on the viewer's right, facing the king (who is the dominant figure in the plaque) on the left side. According to a theory stated elsewhere (Williamson 1969: 220, n. 1), harpists seated on the viewer's right of centre are usually depicted in mirror-image, so that the harp remains in the foreground, fully displayed, and the harpist thus appears to play with his left hand. When shown on the viewer's left (as in the Pyu predella), the harpist plays in 'normal' position with his right hand. Figures depicted in mirror-image will therefore be considered as if in 'normal' position: thus the player's right hand, etc. (as depicted) will be regarded as 'left', and his left as 'right'. In the present example, the resonator of each harp rests on the floor at the side of the harpist under his 'right' elbow, but extends forward and across the 'right' thigh to rest on the 'left' knee, as with the modern harp, so that the strings, attached high near the terminal of the arch are at approximately $45°$ from horizontal. On the largest harp they seem to curve upward, as if far from taut – a phenomenon frequently encountered in harp iconography. The 'right' hand of each harpist appears to be activating the strings on the outside surface, not in the centre (as preferred by modern Burmans) but near the resonator. (This produces a twangy sound on the modern harp.) In the case of Mūsila, on the right, the 'left' arm passes behind the strings to their inside plane, and the hand reappears from the inside to grasp the arch about half-way up, where the remains of three or four fingers, from knuckle to tip, are perhaps visible on the outside. Thus he balances his large instrument against fingers of the 'left' hand, as occurs to some degree on the modern harp. The performance of Guttila (left) is less clear. Cracks in the plaque tend to mislead the eye. However, there is a fragmentary horizontal striation on the arch at about the same position as on that of the larger harp, though it may be that his 'left' elbow bends the other way. Perhaps Guttila (following instructions from Sakka above?) is breaking the strings.

The lower harps seem to represent an entirely different tradition from that of Figures 2 and 3, and perhaps the third harp above. They are larger and crescent-shaped, and have thick arches with no recurving extension beyond the string attachments. If the artisans who carved them were Mon, I believe the harps were also.

Figure 5

**Shwézigôn Guttila-plaque (A.D. *c.* 1086): see Figure 5**[7]

The Shwézigôn pagoda was begun by Aniruddha and completed after his death by Kyanzittha 'in seven months and seven days' (*Glass Palace Chronicle*: 108–10). Jātaka plaques, this time in green-glazed terracotta, were placed around the terraces. In the rush to finish the plaques 'rival

7 Luce 1970, III: pl. 174d; 1969, I: pp. 267–74. Archaeological Survey of India 1913–14; photo neg. 1205. Size: 14½ inches wide, 13½ inches high.

workshops' were probably involved, resulting in a mixed sequence and some duplications (Luce 1969, I: 271 and 273).

In both the harps seen in Figure 5, the junction between arch and resonator is clearly shown. The arch at left emerges almost horizontally from the shallow end of a scoop-shaped resonator, and mounts gradually upward (longer than the resonator) to recurve and taper gracefully at shoulder height. Three or four strings are attached so that the topmost should have reached the terminal of the arch at approximately 30° from horizontal. The right-hand harp is fitted into a smaller space. The structure is the same, but foreshortened so that the arch rises more acutely and matches the resonator in length. The strings mount at approximately 45° from horizontal, as in the Paunggu harp.

The harpists Guttila and Mūsila are seated on the right hand side of the composition, facing the enthroned king on the left; therefore the playing position is reversed. Their feet are tucked behind in Pagán style. Guttila, who is here deified by a halo and an umbrella above, cradles his harp in a way reminiscent of Samudragupta on his coin (Becker 1967: pl. V(a)), the resonator balanced along his 'right' thigh, its deep end projecting slightly upward from under his 'right' elbow, which seems to rest on the surface of the resonator. The 'right' hand plucks the strings nearer the centre, on the outside surface. In one case, perhaps, the 'left' hand hangs from a finger placed on the top string from the inside, in position to play drone tones or change pitch, as in modern practice.

The harps of this plaque are very different from the large crescent-shaped harps that came immediately before and after (West Hpetleik and Nagayôn). In size (relative to the player) they compare with the small Pyu and Paunggu harps; there are points of similarity with modern playing practice. Nevertheless, perhaps this plaque came from one of Kyanzittha's 'rival work-shops' where the artisans were influenced by an Indian tradition that would account for resem-blances to the Samudragupta coin.

## Nagayôn predellas (A.D. *c.* 1090): see Figures 6a and 6b[8]

About four years later (and twenty years after the Hpetleik pagodas), Kyanzittha completed the Nagayôn temple at Myinpagán, a site to which he had fled from oppression in his youth, and where he had been protected while sleeping, by the spread hood of a Nāga (*Glass Palace Chronicle*: 108). The temple is in Mon style with an inner shrine surrounded by a corridor, which is lined on both sides with seated Buddhas in stone relief. The predellas below each of twenty-seven Buddhas who preceded Gotama show the previous lives of Gotama at the moment he received the prophecy of Buddhahood from the then presiding Buddha. Figure 6a shows him as Atula, the Nāga king, playing his harp in adoration before Sumana Buddha; in Figure 6b, as Sakka Purindada, he plays the harp before Dhammadassi Buddha. These harps seem to stem

8    Luce 1970, III: pl. 195d and 198c; 1969, I: pp. 311–21; 1969, II: pp. 105–6.

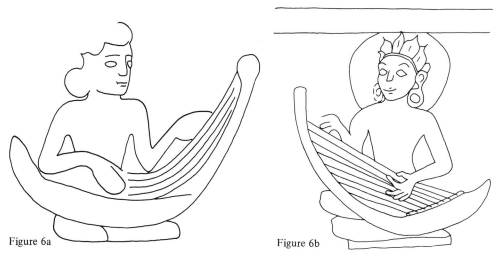

Figure 6a                          Figure 6b

directly from the West Hpetleik harps, at least in crescent-shaped contour, but in these stone-carved examples some structural features are more apparent.

Except for string attachments (high on the arch in Figure 6a), Figure 6b duplicates – in reverse – the composition of Figure 6a. This lends credence to the reversal theory in Burma, since they appear in the same temple. On further investigation it would seem that Kyanzittha's master-plan for this particular temple (painstakingly detailed by Luce) reveals a refinement of the reversal theory. The twenty-seven Buddhas (a predella below each) are placed in alternating niches around the inner and outer walls of the corridor, as shown in the architectural plan in Figure 6c (Luce 1970, III: pl. 186c). This corridor is circumambulated clockwise by the devotee before entering the central shrine. The temple faces north toward the walled city of Pagán. The Buddha series begins in the North Corridor (Luce 1969, I: 314; 1969, II: 105–6), *inner* wall, first niche from the northwest corner, and proceeds clockwise along the inner wall, turns to the right at the northeast corner and again to the right at the southeast corner. The predella shown in Figure 6a is in the first niche on the inner side of the South Corridor, and is on the devotee's right as he approaches, passing from right side to left. Atula Nāgarāja, in the key position on the left side of the composition's centre, faces the approaching devotee, playing his harp in 'normal' position with his right hand. The twenty-seven Buddhas continue in alternate niches along the inner side of the South Corridor (following the text of the *Buddhavaṁsa Khuddaka Nikāya*, according to Luce 1969, I: 314), and the devotee, rounding the southwest corner, enters the West Corridor, where he proceeds to the seventh niche, near the northwest corner. At this point he crosses over to the outer wall of the corridor, continuing the series with the third niche from the corner in the North Corridor, where he proceeds (still clockwise) with a second circumambulation, viewing the predellas of the *outer* wall. Rounding the northeast corner he again enters the East Corridor to face the Dhammadassī Buddha in the first niche on his left. He passes the predella (Figure 6b) from left to right. The Sakka Purindada, in mirror-image on the right-hand side, confronts him as he passes. From this demonstration it is clear that the clockwise circumambulation of the devotee was a factor in the planning of the Nagayôn Jātaka-

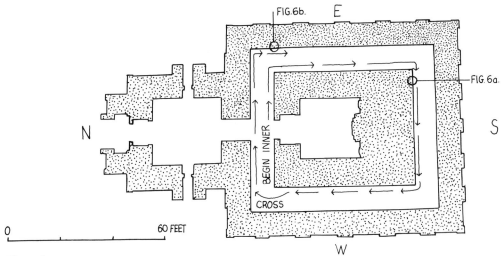

Figure 6c

plaques. In a study of harpists associated with Buddhist temples, the following criteria should be taken into account: (1) whether the devotee passes a painting or sculpture on an inner wall (his right side) or on an outer wall (his left side); (2) whether the dominant figure in the scene, if it be a harpist, faces him as he passes;[9] (3) exactly where, when, and for how long the 'reversal theory' persisted as an artists' convention.

The following observations relate to the predella in Figure 6b, which shows a refinement of detail that could not, in my opinion, be accidental. Though the arch is thick and stumpy as it reaches its terminal, it rises for some little distance above the string attachments, and is longer than the resonator, which it joins in 'orchid spray' style, below and about midway along the shortest string. The resonator is boat-shaped. Though the stern is confused with the drapery knot of the next figure, it is probably in a shallow cup-shape (not as deep as in the modern harp). A new and startling feature ties this harp directly to the modern harp — it has a string-bar clearly visible on the surface of the resonator, and also what appears to be a hump, similar to the modern 'monkey head'. The strings are cut precisely. They number eight, mounted between string-bar and arch at about 40° to the string-bar. There is one possible cord-encirclement of the arch at the attachment of the shortest string.

The resonator is tilted forward and down so that the stern is considerably above the prow (which is, again, not as deep as that of the modern harp). This rests well back over the 'left' thigh; at mid-section it may touch the floor. The stern seems to rest on the knee of the next figure. The arch terminal is now at shoulder level, and the strings at about 35° from horizontal (compare the modern position, Plate 1).

The fingers of the 'left' hand seem to rest on the top string from behind and near the arch.

9  Both Guttila-plaques described above (Figures 4 and 5) are on inside walls. However, in the composition of each scene, the king (who may represent the then-reigning Buddha) is the dominant figure who faces the devotee. The harpists, in smaller scale, and on the right of the scene, face the king in mirror-image.

The 'right' thumb, forefinger and third finger are in motion to activate the strings on their out-side surface, not quite in the centre of the strings. The third finger seems to be extended to damp as in modern practice. In modern playing the thumb normally would pluck the topmost strings, the forefinger the lower (see Plate 1).

I believe this predella proves that local (not imported) artists were deeply involved at the Nagayôn, and that this particular individual had observed closely both the instrument and how it was played. If, as Luce suggests (1969, I: 182), the artists were suddenly ordered by Kyanzittha to depict many new subjects in stone, they must have had a look at real models before beginning to work, especially in the case of the harp, which is difficult to draw let alone carve. They cut the harps as well as they could in the tiny spaces allotted in the predellas, achieving some details — such as the strings, string-bar and fingers in this case — amazingly well.

In the same temple there is a painting illustrating the Guttila Jātaka with an Old Mon gloss: *Bodhisat das tin miṅ tana* ('The Bodhisat was a player on the harp') — *tana* meaning 'harp', the Old Mon name for this instrument.[10]

## Predellas of the Nanda Temple (A.D. *c.* 1105): see Figures 7a and 7b[11]

The Nanda — or Ānanda, in Mon style — was the last and greatest of Kyanzittha's temples. The outer corridor holds eighty sculptured stone plaques illustrating the life of Gotama up to his Enlightenment. Beneath the reclining Prince, a predella shows four women musicians playing harp (Figure 7a) and flute, singing, and playing bamboo clapper. Figure 7b is from a scene showing the Prince in *dhyānamudrā* with the same women sprawled asleep below, their aban-doned instruments shown in silhouette in the centre. The two scenes are depicted in adjoining niches and complement each other.

In Figure 7a the harp follows the general crescent-shape of the Hpetleik and Nagayôn harps (Figures 4, 6a, 6b). The arch is more slender, and probably recurves gracefully to reach the level of the harpist's headdress; it equals the resonator in length and joins it in 'orchid spray' style. This is clearly shown in Figure 7b. The heavy resonator, completely visible only in Figure 7a, is boat-shaped, and now of considerable bulk in the mid-section, with higher prow and shallow pointed stern. Though the strings are treated *en masse* with no attempt at delineation, it is clear that they are now attached lower down on the arch, a detail better seen in Figure 7b than in Figure 7a.

Seated on the far left side of the predella, the harpist in Figure 7a holds her harp in 'normal' (rather than reverse) position. She sits with feet tucked under, holding the harp very high on her right hip. The prow is tilted downward over her left thigh, the stern in a higher position, hugged by her right elbow. The strings are thus close to the angle of the strings in modern play-

10   Letter from Professor Luce, 27 November 1972.
11   Luce 1970, III: pl. 287a, 287b; 1969, I: pp. 357–73; also Becker 1967: pl. V(b). Size: 40 inches high, 22 inches wide.

ing position. The left hand is not visible, except perhaps as a bulge supporting the arch. The right hand rests on the surface of the resonator in position to pluck with thumb and forefinger on the outside surface of the strings. The whole position of the harp looks uncomfortably high (compare Plate 1).

### Lokahteikpan Temi Jātaka (A.D. 1113–c. 1155): see Figure 8[12]

This temple was built in the Transition Period when the style of architecture and also that of calligraphy was changing from Mon to Burmese. The interior of this temple, entered by a vestibule, is now an open continuous vaulted unit, the large wall spaces decorated with paintings, their descriptive glosses in Old Mon as well as Old Burmese script (sometimes both in the same inscription). The inscription (Bohmu Ba Shin 1962: 91) of the painting from which Figure 8 is taken is in Old Burmese: *Purhalon con nhen phlan e cam e*. It may be transcribed in modern Burmese (Standard Conventional Transcription: Okell 1971: 66–7) thus: *Hpayà laùng saùng hnyìn hpyìn sàn i*. It is translated (Bohmu Ba Shin 1962: 64): '[They] test the Bodhisatta with harp and trumpet.' This is the earliest appearance of the Old Burmese word *con* (*saùng*), meaning 'harp'. Bohmu Ba Shin dates the inscriptions, on the basis of the orthography and calligraphy, and on the style of architecture and paintings of the temple, to the reign of Cañsū I (Alaùng-si-thu), A.D. 1113–c. 1155.[13] (Luce dates the temple A.D. c. 1125: 1969, I: 385.)

The arch of this harp is somewhat ambiguous. It appears to be short and thick, terminating abruptly in a bulbous knob at shoulder level (cf. Becker 1967: fig. 6). The back of the resonator is obscured by the figure in front (who should be playing the hnyin); the front is shaped like the modern resonator, without the decorative loop (hsahtò: see p. 212). There are three or four strings, and several tuning cords are visible on the arch, with what are perhaps their tassels dangling close to the outside of the arch.

Playing position is reversed, since the harpist sits to the right of centre. The resonator is in horizontal position resting along the 'right' thigh of the player. The strings rise at about 40°.

A flaking of paint has obscured the 'left' hand, which may have rested near (or behind) the knob of the arch. The 'right' hand is in position to pluck the strings in the centre of their length.

Another interpretation of the arch might be attempted by following the dark curve from its 'orchid spray' insertion in the resonator to the point where it recurves sharply in a pointed shape somewhat like a bo leaf (as in the modern harp). The line of the prow is distinctly Burmese, and tuning cords (with a few tassels) may be seen for the first time.

The examples included up to this point sketch, I believe, a pattern of evolution in the representations of arched harps in Burma. The mid-seventh-century Pyu harp from Śrī Ksetra is linked

---

12   Bohmu Ba Shin 1962: pl. 34, pp. 64 and 91.
13   Letter from John Okell, May 1975, with photograph by Paul Fox of SOAS.

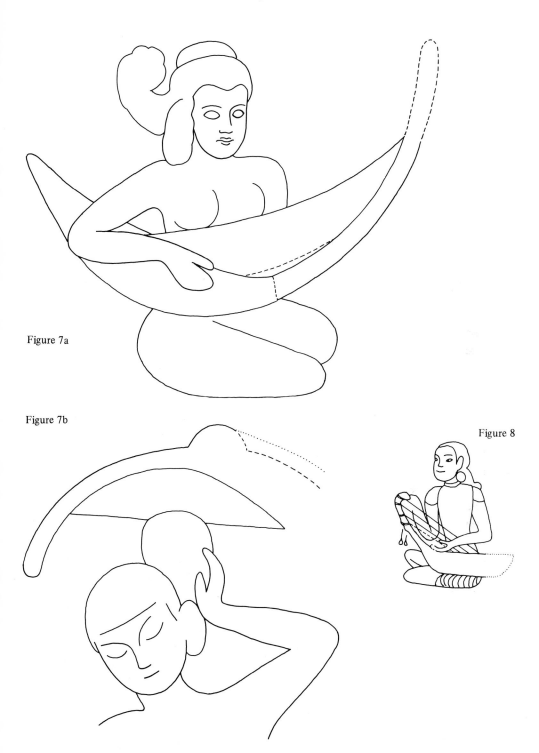

Figure 7a

Figure 7b

Figure 8

tenuously to Pagán through the small Paunggu harp, found in a mid-eleventh-century temple. Later harps of the same relative size are shown in the Guttila-plaque of the Shwézigôn (*c.* 1086), with similarity to the Paunggu harp in Mùsila's harp, and perhaps some Indian influence recognisable in Guttila's. More important, however, are the large crescent-shaped harps of the West Hpetleik pagoda (*c.* 1070), which reflect a strong, fresh tradition, probably Mon, through the Mon craftsmen who are thought to have carved them. This general style is continued in the Nagayôn temple (*c.* 1090), where an artists' convention regarding the depiction of harps in Pagán is demonstrated. One Nagayôn harp also exhibits features of construction and of playing style which link it directly to the modern harp and modern performance technique. The harp, twice shown in adjoining niches at the Ānanda temple (*c.* 1105), adds grace and senuous beauty to this pictorial evolution, as well as some sophistication of the heavy boat-shaped resonator and refinement of the arch. A truly Burmese prow (as yet without hsahtò), with a number of strings attached by tuning cords to the poorly preserved arch, characterise the painted harp from the Lokahteikpan temple (*c.* 1125). Several small tassels dangling from the cords seem visible to the discerning eye.

## Later developments

To help fill in the gap between medieaval Pagán (*c.* 850–1287) and modern Mandalay (from 1857), there is a fresco, published in a volume illustrating Burmese dance,[14] which shows an eleven-stringed harp and other instruments accompanying an *Anyein* dance (see Figure 9), said to date from the Ava dynasty (1364–1555). From a recent study of Burmese wall-painting, the style would seem to resemble that of the mid eighteenth century (Bailey 1978: figs. 12, 18; pp. 46–8). The stylised harp has a recurved arch (not as long as the resonator) with a sharply turned terminal carved to represent a bo leaf, which is characteristic of the modern harp. The arch seems to protrude from prow end of the curved resonator (not characteristic). It bears eleven strings which are attached to the lower half of the arch, but no tuning cords or tassels are visible. The harpist is seated cross-legged, and plays in a caricature of 'normal' position, being placed in the left half of the entire composition. What seems to be an unusually detailed depiction of the left thumb (on the inside surface) raising the pitch of the fourth string from the top is not borne out by the right hand on the outside of the strings playing the sixth string (or the sixth and ninth strings) from the top.

   A second illustration from the same source (no. 170) is from a 'White Parabeik' of the Kònbaung dynasty (1752–1885), probably early or mid nineteenth century, showing a scene from a royal bedchamber, with Anyein dance accompanied by harpist and singer (see Figure 10). The exquisite harp has a slender graceful arch in 'orchid spray' style, widely recurved to show a bo-tree leaf at head level, hanging over the prow of a deep-bowled resonator with a small

14   Published in Rangoon in 1959 during the centenary of the founding of the city of Mandalay: Ù Mìn Naing (ed.), *Pyi daung sú aká padei tha* (The dances of Burma): illustration no. 172.

Figure 9

Figure 10

hsahtò ('ornamental hairpin') attached below the arch (compare Figure 1). The skin has been pierced by two sound holes (there are four in the modern harp). There are six tuning cords with small dangling tassels, therefore six strings, attached fairly high on the arch. The harpist sits with feet tucked under, but the placement of the harp is utterly anomalous: the stern of the resonator is placed forward over the knees of the harpist, while the prow with hsahtò and arch extends beyond her left hip, facing backwards (compare Figure 1)! Nevertheless, the right hand still plucks the strings on the outside surface, though perforce too near the resonator, and the left hand is in the proper position behind the strings. These entertainers are placed at the extreme right of a long narrow panel; the artist has chosen an ingenious but absurd way of solving his reversal problem by turning the harp unauthentically in order to maintain an authentically right-handed harpist.

A twelve-stringed harp in the Victoria and Albert Museum, long associated with the Burmese crown jewels that were removed from the Mandalay palace in 1885, has extensive raised lacquer and gold-leaf decoration on the skin, particularly on the 'monkey head'. Four sound holes are visible, similar in placement to those of the modern harp. This harp was probably made in

Plate 2. Burmese harp, nineteenth century (courtesy of the Victoria and Albert Museum, London)

Mandalay before 1885. It has a small decorated hsahtò below the arch (Plate 2).

The harp used by Daw Khin Khin Galè in Plate 1 was also made in Mandalay (where she was born at court, the daughter of a government minister). Her harp was made by her harp teacher, Dei-wá Eindá Ù Maung Maung Gyì (1855–1933), the last court harpist. Though he is known to have initiated the use of the fourteenth string, this instrument has only thirteen, made of twisted raw silk with surplus length hanging over the side (easily pulled up to repair breakage). Tiny red tassels decorate the ends of the yellowish strings; the tuning cords also have small tassels. There is quite a large hsahtò, heavily decorated. In the style perhaps of late-nineteenth- and early-twentieth-century harps, the bo-leaf terminal of the arch is decorated with a necklace-like band and gold leaf. The Mandalay harpmaker Ù Hmat Kyee, who made my harp in 1959, preferred to show the beautiful natural eye of the cutch root in the centre of the bo leaf, and to carve the hsahtò in an even larger size. The cord tassels are almost three inches long. It is probable that the size of the hsahtò and cord tassels, as well as the shape of the arch, the decoration of its terminal, and the quality and style of the lacquer decoration will be among the criteria for dating harps of the last hundred years or so.

Before closing I should like to offer a possible explanation for the thick arches and stubby terminals of early harp representations in Burma, as compared with the graceful proportions of the modern saùng-gauk. According to a Burmese parabeik translation of unknown date — read to me hurriedly as I was on the point of departing from Burma, and translated orally into English — *pò-mè-za* (or *bò-mè-za*), roughly translated as 'mulberry', was the wood used for the construction of harps until the reign of Bodawpaya (A.D. 1782–1819). It is said that the king asked Ù Sá (later to become Myá-wadi Wun-gyì Ù Sá (1766–1853): see Williamson, in press), who was then said to be playing a harp with only seven strings, to improve the instrument (U Khin Zaw 1941: 725). According to the above parabeik account, he did this in the following reign of Bá-gyì-daw (1819–37). He increased the number of strings to thirteen, and strengthened the construction to accommodate this added stress, perhaps establishing the official templates still used by the harpmaker in Mandalay in 1960. In June 1968, Ù Sein Nyunt, late principal (retired) of the State School of Fine Arts in Mandalay, found pò-mè-za (or bò-mè-za) growing in the Government Botanical Gardens in Maymyo, Burma, under the botanical name *Albizia chinensis* (bohmeza).[15] In Lace and Rodger (1961: 5)[16] the heartwood is described as small, soft and not durable, used for such things as domestic utensils and 'rough turnery' such as *pwè* drums. Perhaps it was Ù Sá who changed the wood used in the harp to padauk heartwood (*Pterocarpus macrocarpus*) for the resonator and cutch root (*Acacia catechu*) for the arch. These are the woods used in the modern harp (Williamson 1968: 47–8). Cutch root has the advantage of greater tensile strength, permitting a slender diameter, and is apt to grow in a beautiful natural curve when located on the side of a hill (Williamson 1975: 112). If the stem-wood of pò-mè-za had been used for the large crescent-shaped Pagán harps with seven or eight strings (Figures 4, 6a, 6b, 7a, 7b), an arch of thicker proportions would have been required to prevent cracking under the stress of tuning. Extension above string attachments with a recurve (which in the modern harp is purely decorative) would scarcely have been practicable, although a recurve was evidently possible on smaller harps (Figures 2, 3, 5).

There are, obviously, large gaps in this sampling of harp iconography and history in Burma. From the Pyu harp of the mid seventh century to the earliest representation in Pagán (mid eleventh century) is already four hundred years, broken only by the account in the *Xin Tangshu* of A.D. 802. There follows a rapid sequence of examples from Early Pagán, all dated within the span of a century (c. 1050–1150). Then, if 'Ava dynasty' is to be taken literally, a gap of four centuries (c. 1150–1555); or, if not, the tremendous gap of about six or seven centuries to the Kònbaung dynasty (1752–1885). A part of that long period may never be accounted for, because of cultural blackouts that seem to have occurred in Burma. In poetry there is nothing of note from c. 1630 to 1730 (Hlá Pe 1971: 64); in wall-painting there seems to be no identified record for a period of four hundred years, between the close of the thirteenth century at Pagán

15   Letter from Ù Sein Nyunt, 7 June 1968.
16   Letter from Professor Luce, 26 August 1972.

and the wall paintings of Sagaing and Pagán of the late seventeenth and eighteenth centuries respectively. The sequence of existing wall paintings does consistently show, however, that Jātaka-scenes and scenes from the life of Gotama were always depicted in terms of contemporary life in the Burma of their own period (Bailey 1978: 60–1). It is logical to infer, therefore, that the same truth applies to the arched harps appearing in them.

On the linguistic side it should be noted that the Sanskrit word *vīṇā*, used for the arched harp in ancient India, never occurs in any of the languages of Burma. Only the Old Mon name *tana* and the Old Burmese *coṅ* (*saùng*) have thus far been recorded.[17] This tends to weaken the argument that the Burmese harp came directly from India, and leaves the question of origin or provenance open for Burmese scholars themselves to solve when it is possible for them to excavate important archaeological sites, or when studies can be expanded at already known sites.

17   Letters from Professor Luce, 27 February 1972 and 17 April 1972.

## Bibliography

Bailey, Jane Terry 1978. 'Some Burmese paintings of the seventeenth century and later', part II, *Artibus Asiae* XL: pp. 41–61, Ascona
Bohmu Ba Shin 1962. *Lokahteikpan*, Burma Historical Commission, Rangoon
Becker, Judith 1967. 'Migration of the arched harp from India to Burma', *Galpin Society Journal* XX: pp. 17–23 and plates
*Glass Palace Chronicle*. Pe Maung Tin and G.H. Luce, translators, *Glass Palace Chronicle of the Kings of Burma*, London 1923 / Rangoon 1960
Groslier, Bernard 1957. *Angkor*, London
Hlá Pe 1971: 'Burmese poetry (1300–1971)', *Journal of the Burma Research Society* LIV part 2: pp. 59–114, Rangoon
Khin Zaw 1941. 'Burmese music: a preliminary account', *Bulletin of the School of Oriental and African Studies* X part 3
Lace, J.H. and Alex Rodger 1961. *List of trees . . . from Burma*, 3rd edn, London
Le May, Reginald 1954/6. *The culture of South-east Asia*, London
Luce, G.H. 1969–70. *Old Burma – Early Pagán*, vols. I–III, New York
Marcel-Dubois, Claudie 1941. *Les instruments de musique de l'Inde ancienne*, Paris
Mìn Naing, B.A. 1959. *Pyi daung sú aká padei tha*, Rangoon
Morton, David 1976. *The traditional music of Thailand*, Los Angeles
Okell, John 1971. *A guide to the romanization of Burmese*, London
Stern, Theodore, and Theodore A. Stern 1971. 'I pluck my harp: musical acculturation among the Karen of Western Thailand', *Ethnomusicology* XV no. 2: pp. 186–219
Williamson, Muriel C. 1968. 'The construction and decoration of one Burmese harp', *Selected Reports in Ethnomusicology* I no. 2: pp. 45–72, Los Angeles
Williamson, Muriel C. 1969. 'Les harpes sculptées du Temple d'Ishtar à Mari', *Syria* XLVI fasc. 3–4: pp. 208–25
Williamson, Muriel C. 1975. 'A supplement to the construction and decoration of one Burmese harp', *Selected Reports in Ethnomusicology* II no. 2: pp. 111–15, Los Angeles
Williamson, Muriel C., in press. 'A biographical note on Myá-wadi Wung-gyì Ù Sá', *Musica Asiatica* II, Oxford

# An Anglo-Saxon harp and lyre of the ninth century

GRAEME LAWSON

It was as recently as 1972 that musicological attention was first drawn to the presence of a stringed musical instrument on the face of the ninth-century Anglo-Saxon sculpted column at Masham, North Yorkshire. In *Antiquity* XLVI, R.N. Bailey identified one of the panels in the third series of arcaded scenes as a portrayal of King David the Psalmist together with three supporting figures (Bailey 1972; also Wright 1967). He observed that David was playing a round-lyre not unlike the recently reconstructed Sutton Hoo instrument (Bruce-Mitford 1970) and that this was the only occurrence of such a scene among surviving pre-Norman carvings in England.[1]

The monument, as it now stands in the churchyard at Masham, is incomplete. It is cylindrical and of fairly massive proportions, having a length of 2.06 m from its base to the truncation bisecting its fourth and uppermost pictorial band. Collingwood, publishing in 1907, considered it to be the base of a large cross-shaft, and although this is now seen to be rather less certain,[2] it does not appreciably affect the interpretation of the iconography. Of more consequence was his failure to recognise the identity of the David-scene itself, since the acceptance of his report as the definitive account of the monument may have been largely responsible for the subsequent neglect of its musicological potential (Collingwood 1907, 1927). The relatively poor condition of the monument's surface, which was probably the cause of this initial interpretative failure, is due to considerable weathering resulting from its complete exposure to the elements. Any stucco or paint that may originally have been applied does not survive, and neither does it seem likely that any of the original stone surface remains. Nevertheless there is still a remarkable depth to the relief, and its modern condition by no means precludes identification (Figure 1). In their representation of the extent of erosion Collingwood's published sketches are now seen to be quite misleading.

The existence of David-iconography at Masham is attributable to the presence of what is, for Northumbria, a rather rare sequence of scenes from the Old Testament (Bailey 1972). Elsewhere in early English sculpture David-scenes are still far from common, despite their frequent appearance in the decoration of contemporaneous high crosses in Ireland (Roe 1949), and indeed no

---

1  I am indebted to Dr Bailey for his comments on many aspects of this monument.
2  R.N. Bailey, personal correspondence.

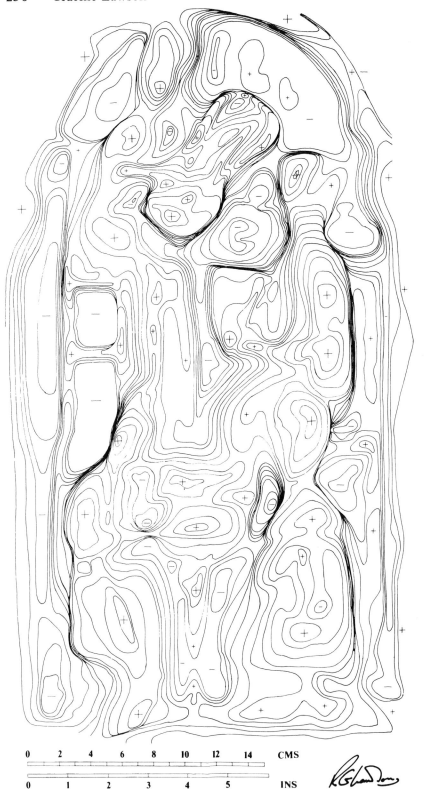

Figure 1. The Masham David-scene: plan of surface detail. Contours are at *c.* 3 mm (1/8 inch)

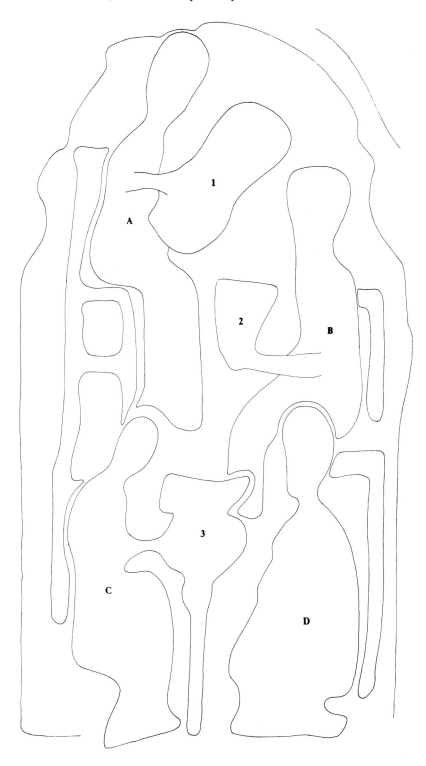

Figure 2. The Masham David-scene: the various features isolated (see Figure 1, opposite)

other English example is at present known to date from before A.D. *c.* 1000. Even in manuscript art few Anglo-Saxon examples remain, although a rather larger sample is known of European and later English illustrations, among which David, his assistants and various stringed and other instruments frequently recur. It is against this iconographic background that the identification of the individual components of the Masham scene must be considered.

Altogether four human figures can be isolated from the mass of features present on the panel (Figure 2, A–D). They are distinguishable on the basis of the clear association between each body and its distinct head and neck, and they are distributed fairly symmetrically on the panel, facing in towards its central axis. Within this central region are three further features which appear to be closely associated with figures A–C (Figure 2, 1–3). There is no fourth feature to correspond with figure D, and minor remaining details seem to be merely the frameworks of the border, seats and throne.

King David, forming figure A, dominates the scene from the upper left quarter, where he sits enthroned with his arm(s) outstretched to contact feature 1. The latter is clearly a round-lyre of contemporaneous Germanic type, as has already been noted, and the identity of the player is implied both by his commanding position and by his possession of this instrument, which is the principal attribute of David as Psalmist in early mediaeval Christian iconography, until A.D. *c.* 1000. The significance of the three supporting figures, B–D, has until now remained unclear, mainly because of the indistinct nature of their preservation and consequent uncertainties surrounding the identification of their two associated features, 2–3.

The second figure, like that of the Psalmist, is also seated, and is positioned in the upper right quarter of the panel, slightly lower than David and facing into the centre of the scene (Figure 2, B). It bears a close association, by an outstretched hand/arm contact similar to that connecting David with feature 1, with a second and smaller feature (Figure 2, 2). This, having an approximately triangular shape, may suggest interpretation as a small triangular harp. Parallels for the occurrence of this instrument at such an early date are not yet known in any English context, but may be seen in the harps drawn in certain contemporaneous Continental manuscript-depictions of David (Figure 3). The widely varying sizes of some of these, contrasting with the tidy conformity of both later pictures of harps and contemporaneous pictures of lyres, may perhaps be due to errors in execution rather than to actual variation;[3] similar defects also occur in representations of their detailed components. The small size of feature 2 need not therefore rule out interpretation as a harp, especially in view of the lack of any wholly satisfactory alternative.

3   Quite possibly resulting from unfamiliarity with the type.

---

Figure 3. European harps in early mediaeval art
A. Ivory cover of the Dagulf Psalter, eighth century (Paris, Louvre)
B. Attic red-figure amphora, fifth century B.C. (London, British Museum)
C. Manuscript, ninth century (Paris, Bibliothèque Nationale, Cod. lat. I, fo. 215v)
D. Manuscript, tenth century (St Gallen, Stiftsbibliothek, Cod. Nr 21, p. 5)
E. Manuscript, late tenth or early eleventh century (Rome, Biblioteca Vaticana, Cod. lat. 83, fo. 12v)
F. Manuscript, early eleventh century (Cambridge, University Library, MS Ff.I.23, fo. 4v)

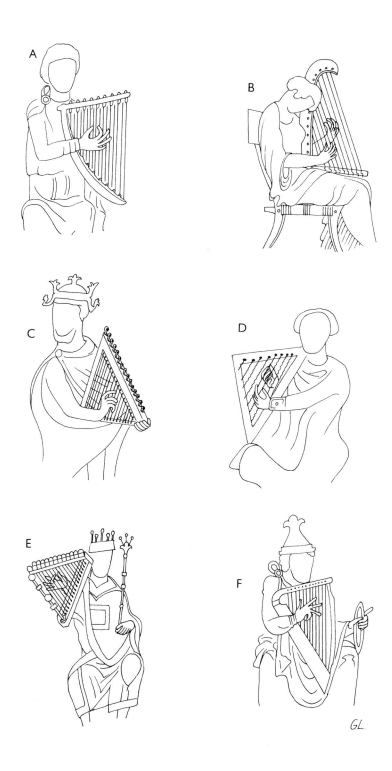

GL.

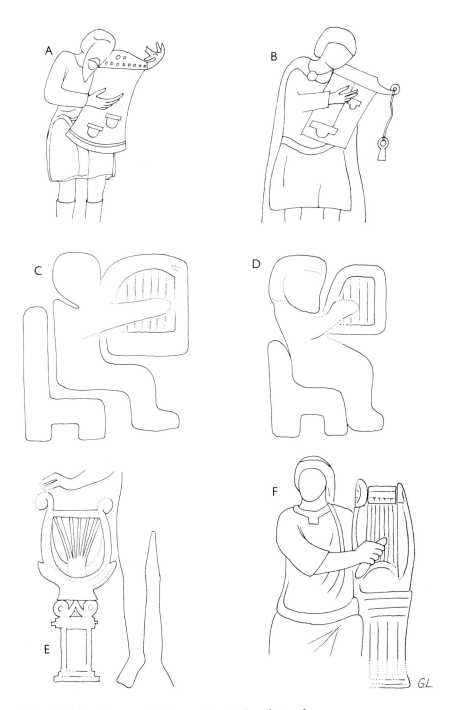

Figure 4. Stringed instruments (?) resembling Masham feature 3
A. Manuscript, eleventh century (Tübingen, Universitätsbibliothek, MS Theol. lat. fol. 358, fo. 1v)
B. Manuscript, eleventh century (Klosterneuburg bei Wien, Stiftsmuseum, Inv. Nr 987, fo. 11v)
C. Relief-sculpture, ninth century (Castledermot, South Cross)
D. Relief-sculpture, ninth century (Castledermot, North Cross)
E. Relief-sculpture, Roman period (Trier, Rheinisches Landesmuseum, Inv. Nr 37.399)
F. Ivory pyxis showing scenes of Achilles, fifth century A.D. (Xanten, Rheinisches Landesmuseum)

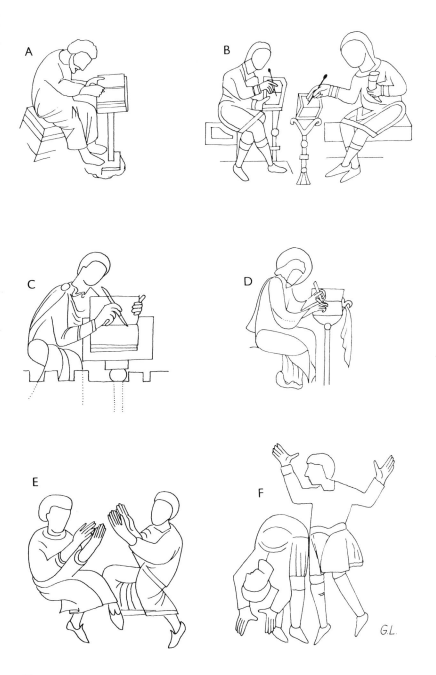

Figure 5. Parallels for the interpretation of the Masham scribe and dancer

A. Ivory book-cover showing David-scene, ninth–tenth century (Paris, Louvre, Inv. Nr MR 373)

B. Manuscript showing David-scene, tenth–eleventh century (Rome Biblioteca Vaticana, Cod. lat. 83, fo. 12v)

C. Manuscript showing David-scene, eleventh century (Munich, Bayerische Staatsbibliothek, CLM 7355, fo. 5v)

D. Manuscript showing St Hilary of Poitiers, eleventh century (Avranches, Bibliothèque Municipale, MS 58, fo. 3v)

E. Manuscript showing David-scene, eighth century (London, British Library, MS Cotton Vespasian A.1, fo. 30v)

F. Manuscript showing David-scene, eleventh century (Tübingen, Universitätsbibliothek, MS Theol. lat. fol. 358, fo. 1v)

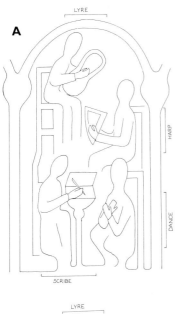

A

LYRE

HARP

DANCE

SCRIBE

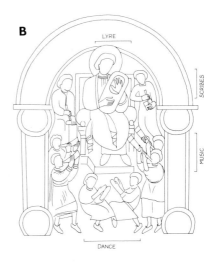

B

LYRE

SCRIBES

MUSIC

DANCE

C

LYRE

DAVID

ACUSABEL

REX

ASAPH

EMAN

AETHAN

IDITHUN

SCRIBES

SCRIBES

D

LYRE

HARP

SCRIBE

E

HARP

DAD

DEXTE
RA DNI

ASAPh

AEMAN

AET
han

IDI
ThUN

SCRIBES

SCRIBES

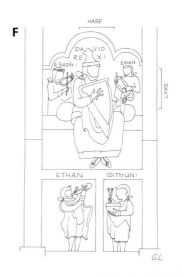

F

HARP

DAVID
REX:

ASAPh:

EMAN

LYRE

ETHAN

IDIThUN:

G.L.

If a musical explanation is suggested for feature 2, the same might be postulated for the third feature, which is similarly associated with the third figure (C), seated in the lower left quarter of the scene. In appearance it is fairly amorphous, but enough shape remains to encourage some attempt at its identification. Indeed at first glance it does seem reminiscent of a number of typologically irregular instruments recorded in various iconographic sources towards and around the end of the first millennium. Foremost among these are the two illustrated (alongside more conventional harps and lyres) in two early-eleventh-century manuscripts at Klosterneuburg and Tübingen (Steger 1961) (Figure 4, A–B); further comparisons might be drawn with some of the equally anomalous instruments of the roughly contemporaneous Irish high crosses (Roe 1949) (Figure 4, C–D). It must be noted, however, that few of these parallels are in themselves of more than doubtful credibility as portrayals of actual chordophones.[4] Furthermore, the presence of a pedestal-like feature supporting feature 3 here, although perhaps paralleled in certain late Roman and Byzantine portraits of Apollo Citharoedus (Figure 4, E–F),[5] is unknown in any such musical context within the more immediate iconography of either the Masham David-scene or these enigmatic Irish and European instruments. In fact the only close parallels for it, within the limits of chronological and geographical acceptability, are all non-musical. Among such parallel scenes can be found the various characteristics of the Masham figure, including his seated position, outstretched arm and inclined head, and in each he is shown writing with a quill pen in an open book set upon a lectern (Figure 5, A–D).[6]

The identification of the third subsidiary figure (Figure 2, D) as a dancer or juggler is the least certain, but is suggested both by his lack of association with any feature comparable with the lyre, harp and lectern forming features 1–3, and by the different, apparently crouching position of his body. This latter, with the contorted position especially of the legs, corresponds in broad terms with others in comparable manuscript-pictures (Figure 5, E–F), bearing in mind that a lack of arm-waving and general flamboyancy here, like the overcrowding observed throughout the panel as a whole, is almost certainly conditioned by the size and medium of the Masham scene (constraints not usually met with in manuscript art). The identification of the first two subsidiary figures also lends weight to a dance-interpretation for this third, for the total composition would then make sense as an economising alternative to David's customary group of four assistants, Asaph, Eman, Ethan and Ithidun (see Figure 6, C–F). These three figures

4  They do not fall readily into any of the three recognised categories (lyre, harp or lute and their subtypes), though they could be misrepresentations, perhaps of classical originals.
5  These, however, are usually much thicker, being derived probably from the small Roman altars which they frequently resemble.
6  It is interesting to note that later in the mediaeval period (around the eleventh and twelfth centuries) early depictions of the European psaltery in David-iconography (which is at that stage virtually their only context) are often difficult to distinguish from lecterns, and that there is consequently some doubt about their identification.

Figure 6. The Masham David-scene: tentative reconstruction, with examples of similar David-groups in north-western European art
A. Masham, North Yorkshire; early ninth century
B. London, British Library, MS Cotton Vespasian A.1, fo. 30v; eighth century
C. Munich, Bayerische Staatsbibliothek, CLM 343, fo. 12v; tenth–eleventh century
D. St Gallen, Stiftsbibliothek, Cod. Nr 21, p. 5; tenth century
E. Rome, Biblioteca Vaticana, Cod. lat. 83, fo. 12v; tenth–eleventh century
F. Cambridge, University Library, MS Ff.I.23, fo. 4v; early eleventh century

together, therefore, may be taken to represent the secondary elements of the iconography of David as Psalmist: accompaniment, transcription and dance (Figure 6, A).

The size of the lyre, estimated from the few available dimensions of the performer, falls within the relatively narrow range confirmed by excavated examples. Its approximate length of 65–70 cm is compatible with the lengths estimated for the published reconstructions of the sixth- or seventh-century Bergh Apton and Sutton Hoo instruments,[7] while the known lengths of the sixth- or seventh-century Oberflacht 31 and eighth-century Cologne P100 instruments at approximately 73 and 52 cm respectively form the concrete outer limits of this range (Paulsen 1972; Fremersdorf 1943). There is similar conformity to this standard size in other lyres depicted elsewhere in the art of the same and adjoining periods and regions, contrasting with the generally more widely varied sizes represented by later examples. The disproportionately large width of the Masham lyre, at around 33 cm, though it disagrees with all extant contemporaneous archaeological data,[8] is however a feature common to virtually all parallels in early mediaeval art (Figure 7). Such a reduced length–width ratio persists and indeed becomes, if anything, even more pronounced in subsequent years, but without any archaeological corroboration it ought probably to be seen as an error in execution.

On the other hand, the apparently 'waisted' curvilinear form of this instrument may well prove to have some basis in fact, and it is this feature that sets it apart from all other surviving first-millennium insular examples.[9] Although it does not represent true waisting (i.e. median narrowing of the resonator, for structural and acoustical purposes), the outward curvature of the arms from the roughly oval body does result in a median narrowing of the instrument as a whole, a shape not attested by any other early English finds or evidence in art, where instruments with straight and parallel sides seem to be the rule. Such curvilinear outlines, however, are almost exclusively the rule on the Continent, both in art and in archaeology, in the latter half of the first millennium, and were subsequently to become common also in late Saxon and

7  These do not survive to their full lengths, but from their remaining proportions they are estimated to have been between 60 and 80 cm in length.
8  No excavated instrument exceeds 20 cm.
9  With the possible exception of the small sixth-century Gilton (Kent) lyre-picture (Bruce-Mitford 1970), and this instrument is rounded rather than strictly waisted.

---

Figure 7. Lyres in north-western European archaeology (A–D) and art (E–L), A.D. 200–1200, to approximately the same scale
A. Lupfen; sixth century
B. Oberflacht 31; sixth–seventh century
C. Sutton Hoo; seventh century
D. Cologne P100; eighth century
E. Hochsheid/Trier, Rheinisches Landesmuseum, Apollo statue; second century
F. Durham, Cathedral Library, MS B.II.30; eighth century
G. Masham, North Yorkshire; early ninth century
H. Cividale, MS CXXXVI; tenth century
I. Klosterneuburg, Stiftsmuseum, MS 987; tenth–eleventh century
J. Munich, Bayerische Staatsbibliothek, MS CLM 7355; eleventh century
K. Cambridge, University Library, MS Ff.I.23; early eleventh century
L. London, British Library, MS Harl. 2804; twelfth century

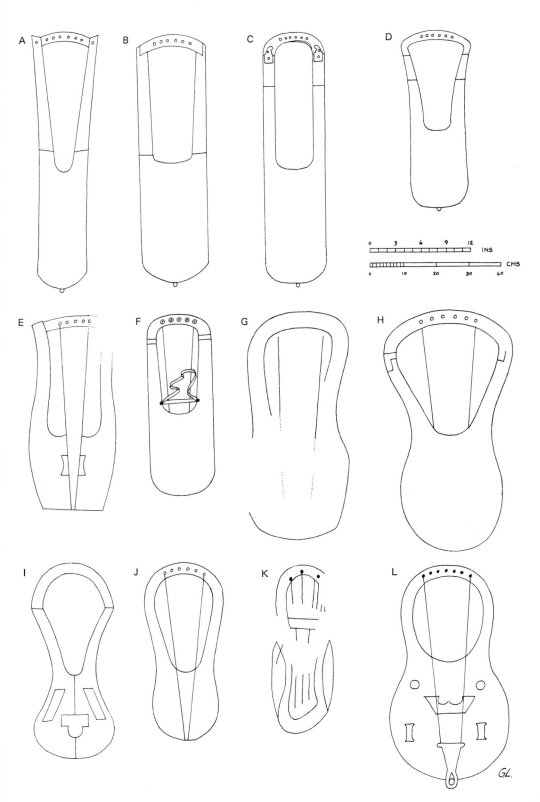

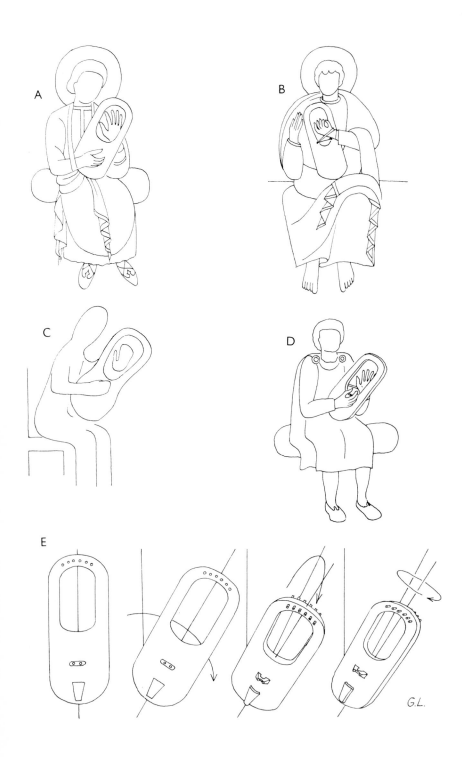

post-Conquest English art. The somewhat exceptional form of the Masham lyre need not, however, imply particularly exceptional circumstances. The small size of the English sample[10] necessitates a cautious approach; and the variety of forms in the continental sample, which includes the remains of one straight- and parallel-sided example,[11] may be taken to imply more general and considerable individuality of design (Figure 7).

David's portrayal in profile, or at least three-quarter profile, is unusual, and affords an opportunity to observe the position of the lyre from a rare vantage-point. We know from the other, almost entirely frontally presented iconographic evidence that the lyre of this period was played resting upon the lap or left thigh of the performer, who was probably normally seated. It was held during performance[12] with the aid of a strap passing around behind his left wrist, and with the long axis of the instrument angled over to his left through between 20° and 40° out of the vertical (Figure 8, A). Further investigation involving experiments with full-size replicas has suggested the likelihood of a secondary angling of the instrument, by rotation around the same axis so as to contact the left hand of the performer more comfortably (Figure 8, D–E). Some confirmation of this has already been noted in an eighth-century illustrated manuscript at Durham, where a slightly different perspective, this time from David's left side, shows much the same arrangement (Figure 8, B).[13] Now the position of the Masham lyre too seems to corroborate the hypothesis, being angled around to face the viewer despite David's own three-quarter or profile position. Of course, it could be argued that its full-face presentation is due to the medium and technique of the relief, but it seems to imply nevertheless that the artist considered a profile of the Psalmist to be quite acceptable alongside an outwardly orientated lyre.

The portrayal of David's accompanist yields little comparable information to assist in the reconstruction of contemporary performance upon the triangular harp. The instrument, if such an interpretation is correct, is being held in much the same position as is the lyre, atop the performer's knees, but its small size and indistinct preservation allow little scope for more detailed assessment. Such irregularity in dimension, appearance and deployment, and an inadequacy in both depiction and preservation, are in fact characteristic of almost all such early pictures of harps, as we have seen (p. 232). Even so, there is at least the suggestion here that, as with the lyre, the player's hands are positioned to either side of the instrument, the right (distant) hand being behind the harp as viewed. This is in keeping with the established techniques

10 This numbers, effectively, no more than ten, including both archaeology and art.
11 The instrument from grave 31 of the Germanic cemetery at Oberflacht, Tuttlingen, West Germany (Paulsen 1972).
12 As distinct from tuning, which is also frequently represented.
13 Durham Cathedral Library MS B.II.30, fo. 81v; this manuscript-illustration also shows the best known example of a wrist-strap (Lawson 1978: 92–5).

---

Figure 8. Anglo-Saxon lyre-playing: evidence for holding-position
A. London, British Library, MS Cotton Vespasian A.1, fo. 30v; eighth century
B. Durham, Cathedral Library, MS B.II.30, fo. 81v; eighth century
C. Masham, North Yorkshire; early ninth century
D. Interpretation based upon A–C and other sources
E. Position of instrument, showing alignment

of later Anglo-Saxon harp-playing, and is quite distinct from that of the later mediaeval triangular or trapezoidal psaltery, in which both hands are invariably applied to the same surface.

It is, however, with the mere existence of such an instrument in ninth-century England that
interest in it mainly lies. The enigma of the instrument named 'hearpe' in Anglo-Saxon literature has recently been tentatively resolved (Bruce-Mitford 1970), and it is now generally equated
with the round-lyres known from archaeological excavations at Sutton Hoo, Taplow, Bergh
Apton and other sites in England and north-western Europe (Lawson 1978). The word itself is
likely to have meant, or rather implied, a current stringed musical instrument, without necessarily having any specific and exclusive association, except by circumstance, with any one particular typological class. Indeed, in later years it came to be applied to various categories of
which one is not even stringed.[14] At some subsequent stage its association in the English
language shifted to the triangular harp, and there is good reason to suspect that this may have
occurred simultaneously with or shortly following the rise of that instrument to pre-eminence
over the traditional lyre. This event is thought to have taken place in the closing years of the
first millennium, a date supported by the triangular harp's domination in manuscript and other
art thereafter, notably but (fortunately) not exclusively in David-iconography.[15] Unfortunately
archaeological confirmation of this date is still lacking, and the origins and early history of the
triangular harp remain largely obscure. Although harps may have been known in Celtic and
Germanic Europe during the earliest mediaeval, Roman and pre-Roman periods, just as they
were in Mediterranean Europe at the same periods, there is no evidence for their having been
anything other than rather rare, alien intrusions into music-cultures whose principal stringed
instruments were lyres.[16] The reasons for this are many and various: forces of tradition die hard
in artefact-evolution, and the complex patterns of relationships between musical instruments
and the musical and cultural ecosystems[17] with which their designs interact (involving musical,
operational, ritual, aesthetic, and technological factors) are considerable pressures for continuity.

From a technological point of view, however, it is interesting to observe that the harp's
finally successful invasion of the lyre's musical territory, both in Britain and in Western Europe,
is accompanied by the introduction into its superstructure of a *fore-pillar*, supporting the pre-

14   The Swedish nyckelharpa ('key-harp') is a partly mechanical instrument of the single-
     necked lute category; the Swedish/Estonian stråkharpa ('bowed harp') is undoubtedly of
     the double-necked lyre category; while the ubiquitous jew's harp (Norwegian and Danish
     mundharpe (lit. 'mouth-harp')) is altogether unrelated to any stringed instrument.
15   For the reversal of the rôles of lyre and harp in David-iconography at around A.D. 1000,
     compare the Masham scene with others shown in Figure 6 above.
16   A remarkable eighth-century portrayal of such a harp is shown on the ivory cover of
     Dagulf's Psalter (Paris, Louvre: Fig. (iii), A), where it appears to possess the characteristics
     of the ancient rather than the modern instrument (the fact that it is being held 'upside-
     down' by ancient standards is important but does not change the identity of the harp at
     all). This ivory is attributed to the Palace School, Aix la Chapelle (Aachen) and shows
     Byzantine influence.
17   For discussion of ecological analogies applicable to the study of musical instruments, see
     Picken 1975: 557–609 and Lawson 1979: ch. 3.

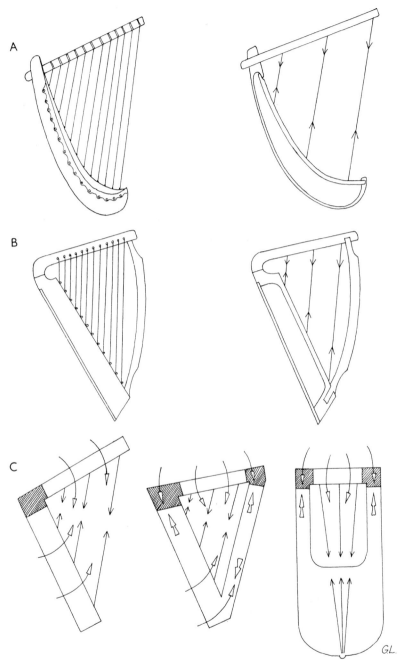

Figure 9. Structural comparison between ancient and mediaeval harps
A. Ancient harp, reconstructed from evidence in Greek red-figure pottery paintings (*c*. 400 B.C.)
B. Anglo-Saxon harp, reconstructed from manuscript and other sources (A.D. *c*. 1050)
C. Schematic diagrams showing stresses in the ancient harp, mediaeval harp and early mediaeval lyre

viously unsupported end of the peg-arm or *neck*. Stress-analysis suggests that this could well be a response to the constraints imposed by the limitations of the indigenous Anglo-Saxon and Germanic (and entirely lyre-based) technology of construction, serving to produce from a harp-design traditionally geared to cantilever principles an instrument with an unprecedented structural affinity to lyres (Figure 9).[18] From a musical standpoint it is also interesting to note that it seems to occur at a time not distant from that of the decline of the Anglo-Saxon and Germanic hearpe-playing minstrel or *scop*, whose wandering or partly wandering rôle may well have been the most significant force for the retention of the light and eminently portable round-lyre during the early Anglo-Saxon period.

The presence of these two instruments on the Masham column, if both interpretations are correct, confirms the simultaneous presence of both the traditional Anglo-Saxon lyre and the new Anglo-Saxon harp, somewhere within the iconographic catchment area of this sculpture, and therefore conceivably within Anglo-Saxon England, as early as the beginning of the ninth century. Continental evidence has for some time suggested that this is feasible for the mainland of north-western Europe at such a date. The Masham instruments now reaffirm the need for a cautious and open-minded interpretation of the archaeological relics of early Anglo-Saxon music.

18   Perhaps the most dramatic effect is the reduction of stress in the main peg-arm/resonator joint. See further Lawson 1979: ch. 6.

## Bibliography

Bailey, R.N. 1972. 'Another lyre', *Antiquity* XLVI

Bruce-Mitford, R.L.S. and Bruce-Mitford, M. 1970. 'The Sutton Hoo lyre, *Beowulf*, and the origin of the frame-harp', *Antiquity* XLIV

Collingwood, W.G. 1907. 'Anglian and Anglo-Danish sculpture in the North Riding of York-shire', *Yorkshire Archaeological Journal* XIX

Collingwood, W.G. 1927. *Northumbrian crosses of the pre-Norman age*, London

Fremersdorf, F. 1943. 'Zwei wichtige Frankengräber aus Köln', *Jahrbuch für Prähistorisch und Ethnographisch Kunst*

Lawson, G. 1978. 'The lyre from grave 22', in B. Green and A. Rogerson (eds.), 'The Anglo-Saxon cemetery at Bergh Apton' (*East Anglian Archaeology*, Report no. 7)

Lawson, G. 1979. 'Stringed musical instruments: artefacts in the archaeology of Northwest Europe 500 B.C.–A.D. 1100', unpublished Ph.D. thesis, Cambridge

Paulsen, P. 1972. 'Leiern', in P. Paulsen and H. Schach-Dörges (eds.), *Holzhandwerke der Almannen*, Stuttgart, pp. 99–107

Picken, L.E.R. 1975. *Folk musical instruments of Turkey*, Oxford

Roe, H.M. 1949. 'The David Cycle in early Irish art', *Journal of the Royal Society of Antiquaries of Ireland* LXXIX

Steger, H. 1961. *David Rex et Propheta*, Nuremberg

Wright, D. 1967. 'The Vespasian Psalter' in *Early English manuscripts in facsimile* no. 14, Copenhagen